ART
LOVE
PASSION

Dogs & Doodles
Volume 1

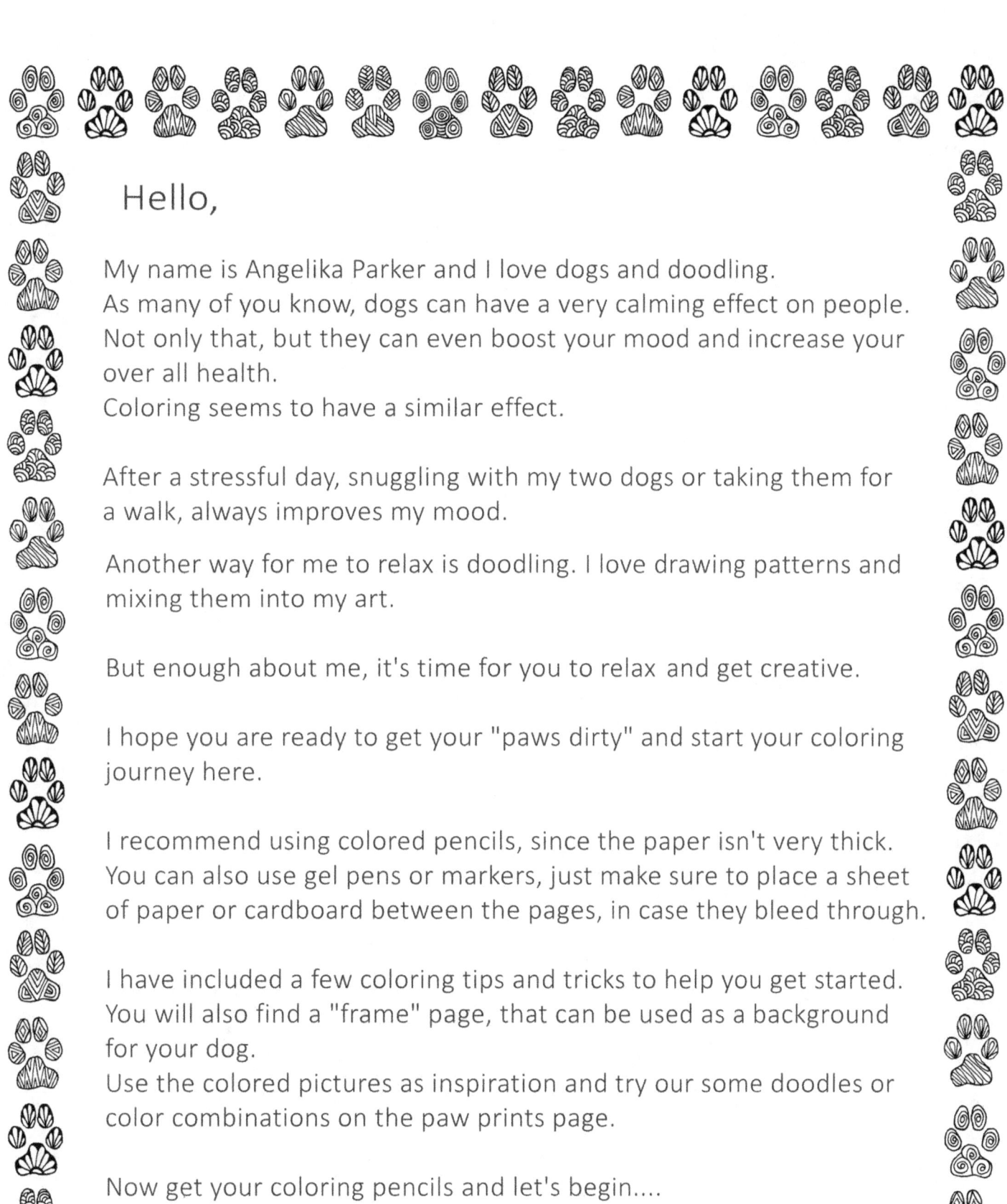

Hello,

My name is Angelika Parker and I love dogs and doodling.
As many of you know, dogs can have a very calming effect on people.
Not only that, but they can even boost your mood and increase your over all health.
Coloring seems to have a similar effect.

After a stressful day, snuggling with my two dogs or taking them for a walk, always improves my mood.

Another way for me to relax is doodling. I love drawing patterns and mixing them into my art.

But enough about me, it's time for you to relax and get creative.

I hope you are ready to get your "paws dirty" and start your coloring journey here.

I recommend using colored pencils, since the paper isn't very thick.
You can also use gel pens or markers, just make sure to place a sheet of paper or cardboard between the pages, in case they bleed through.

I have included a few coloring tips and tricks to help you get started.
You will also find a "frame" page, that can be used as a background for your dog.
Use the colored pictures as inspiration and try our some doodles or color combinations on the paw prints page.

Now get your coloring pencils and let's begin....

Coloring Tips & Tricks

Before you begin coloring, test out your colors on some scrap paper. A lot of times the color on a marker looks very different from the color of that same marker on a piece of paper.
The same goes with colored pencils and gel pens. This will give you a better idea of what your finished piece will look like.

Mixing colors with colored pencils is easier when you use multiple layers. Start with a light layer and keep adding more layers, rather then pressing down hard. Finish your piece by using a colorless blender that will fuse the colors together and will make them look more vibrant.

You can also mix mediums. You could start with a marker and go over it with a colored pencil, or vice versa.

For more tips and tricks, check out some videos online.

Don't be afraid to try out new things. Use the paw prints on this page to make your own doodles, or color combinations.

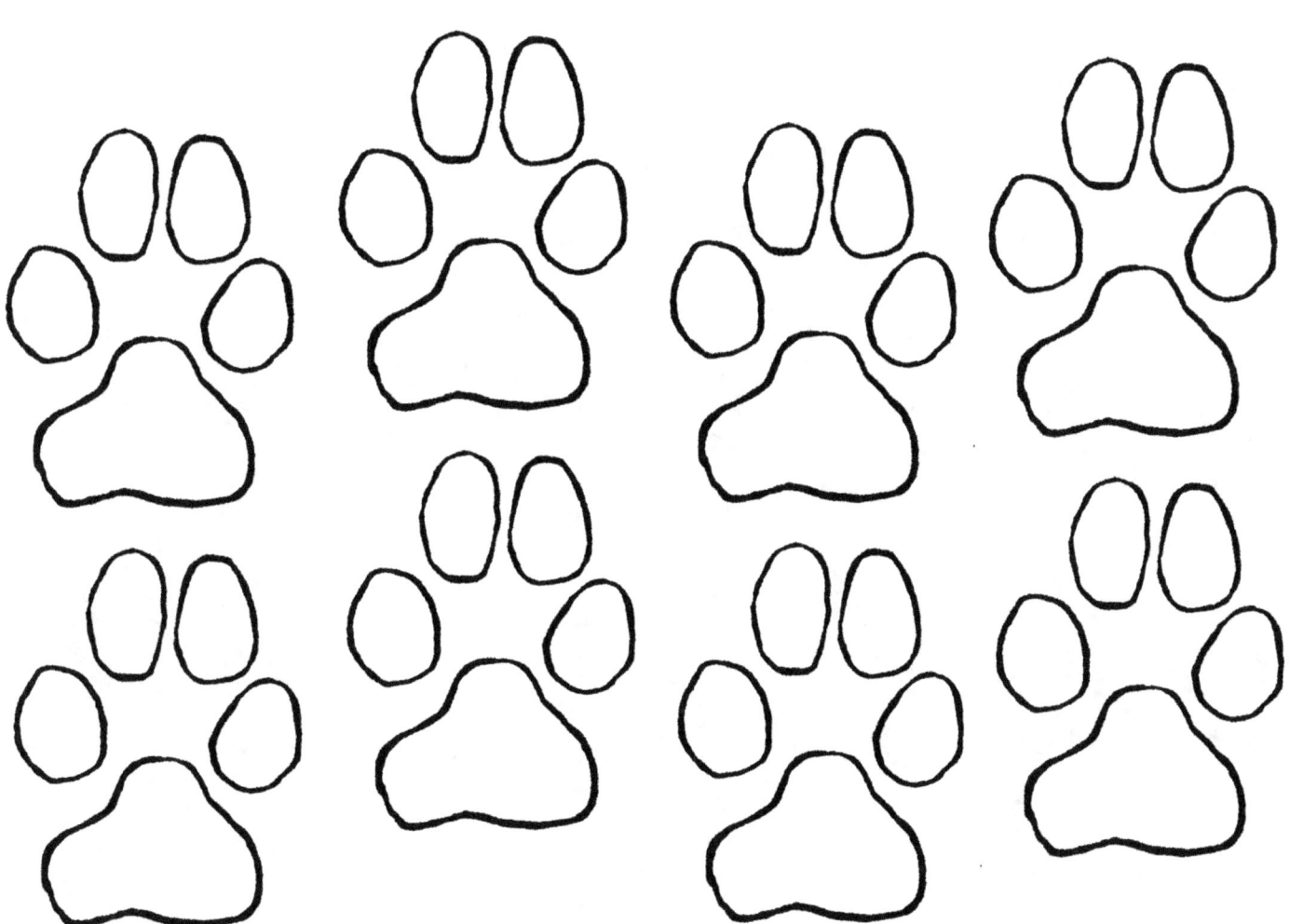

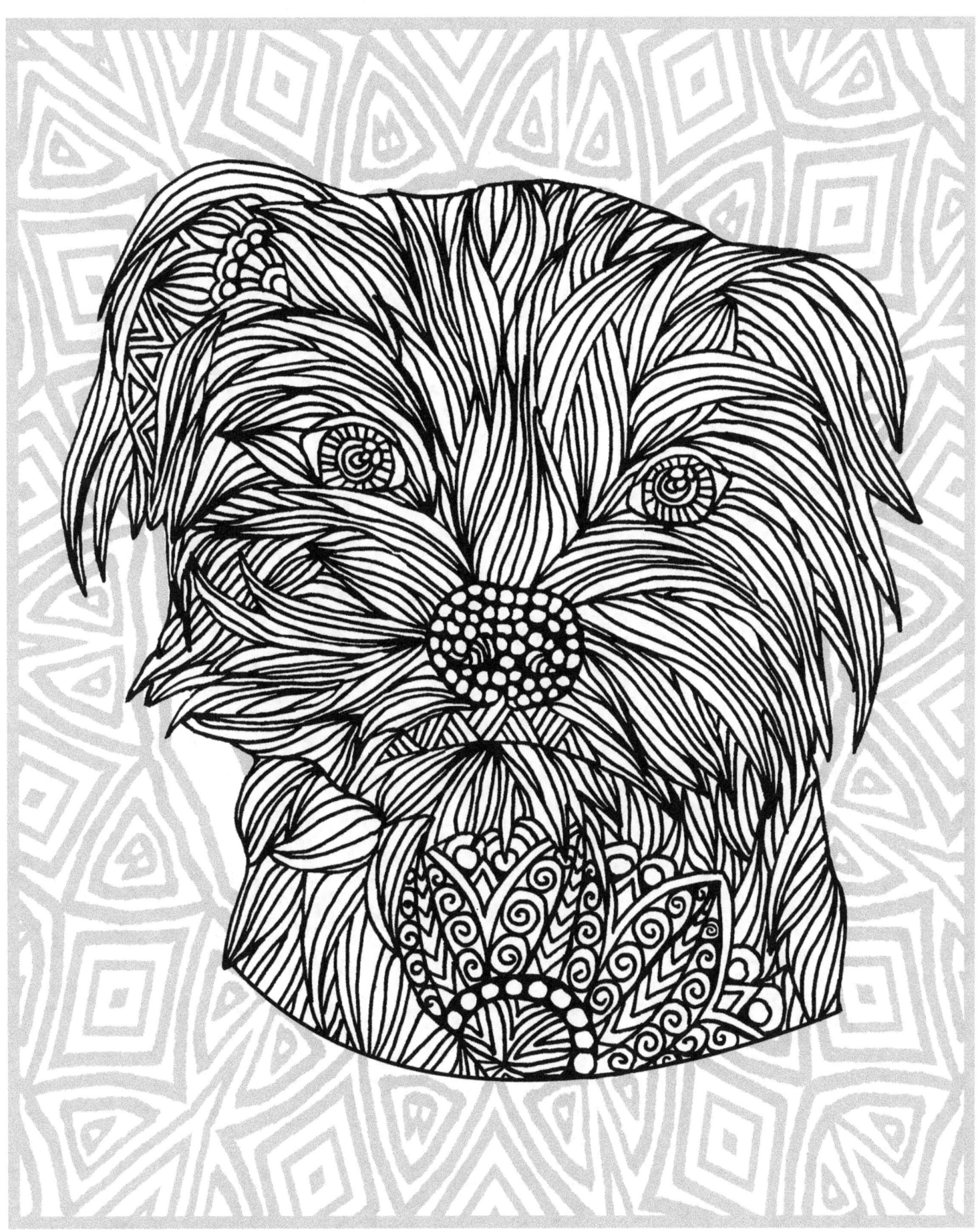

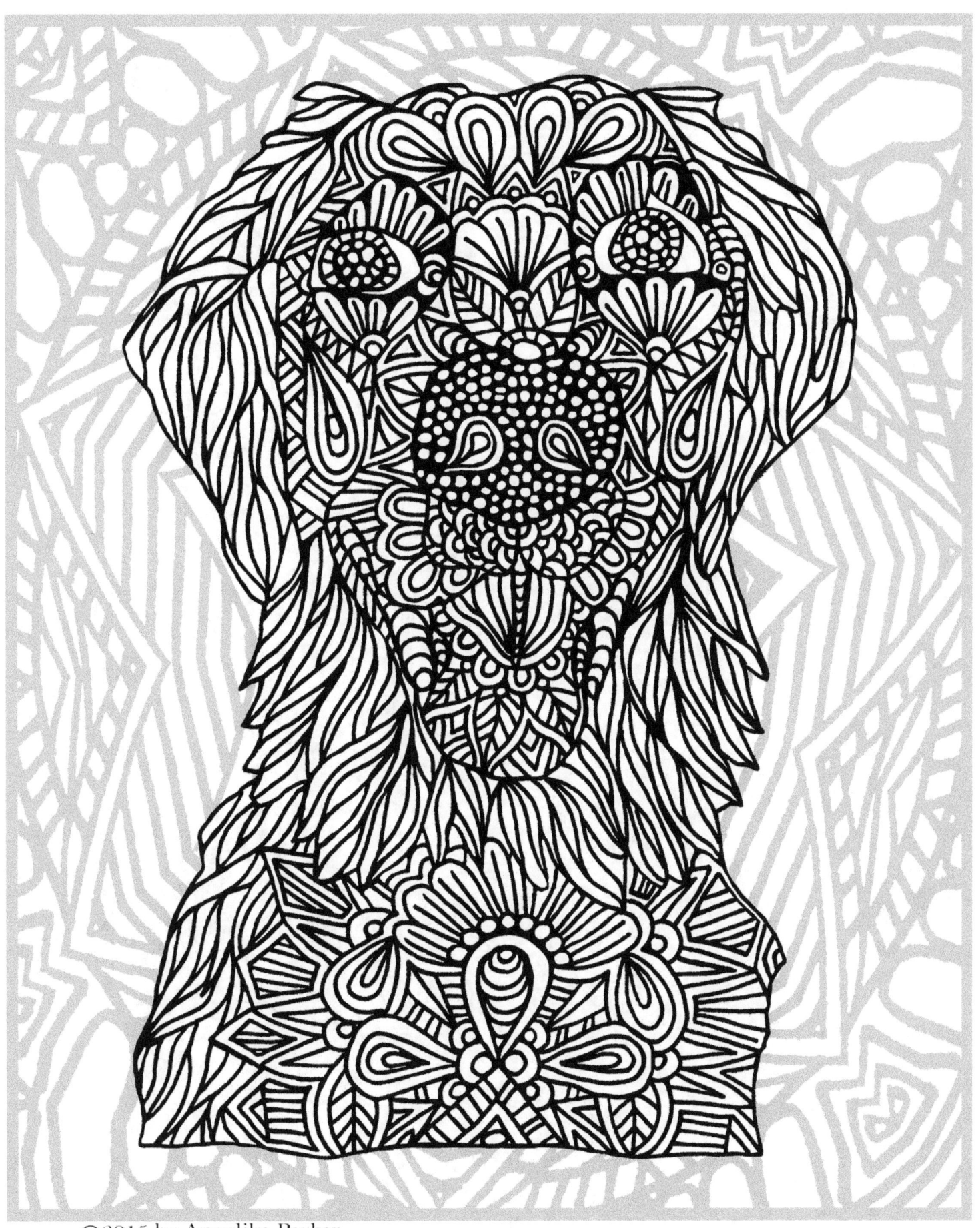

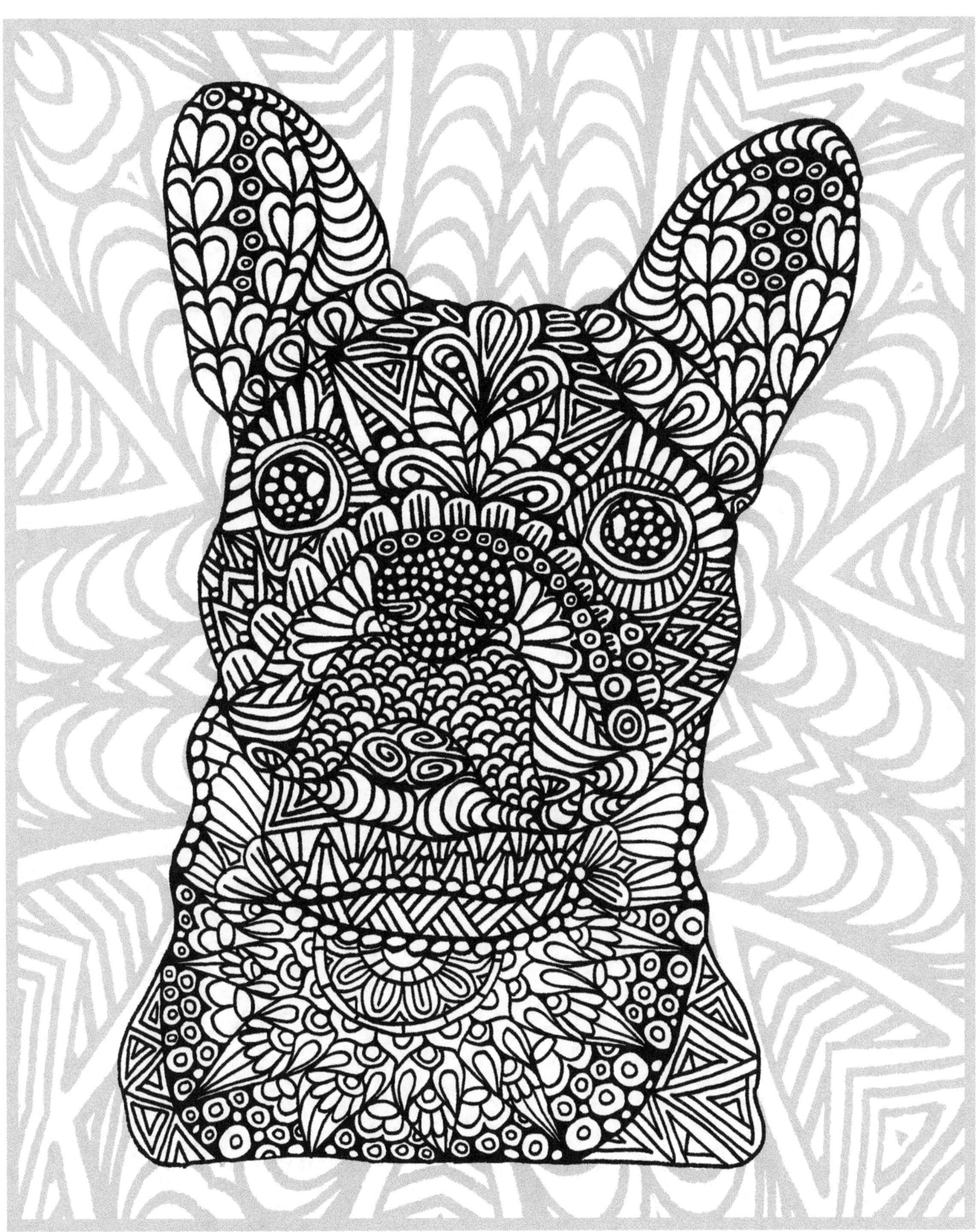

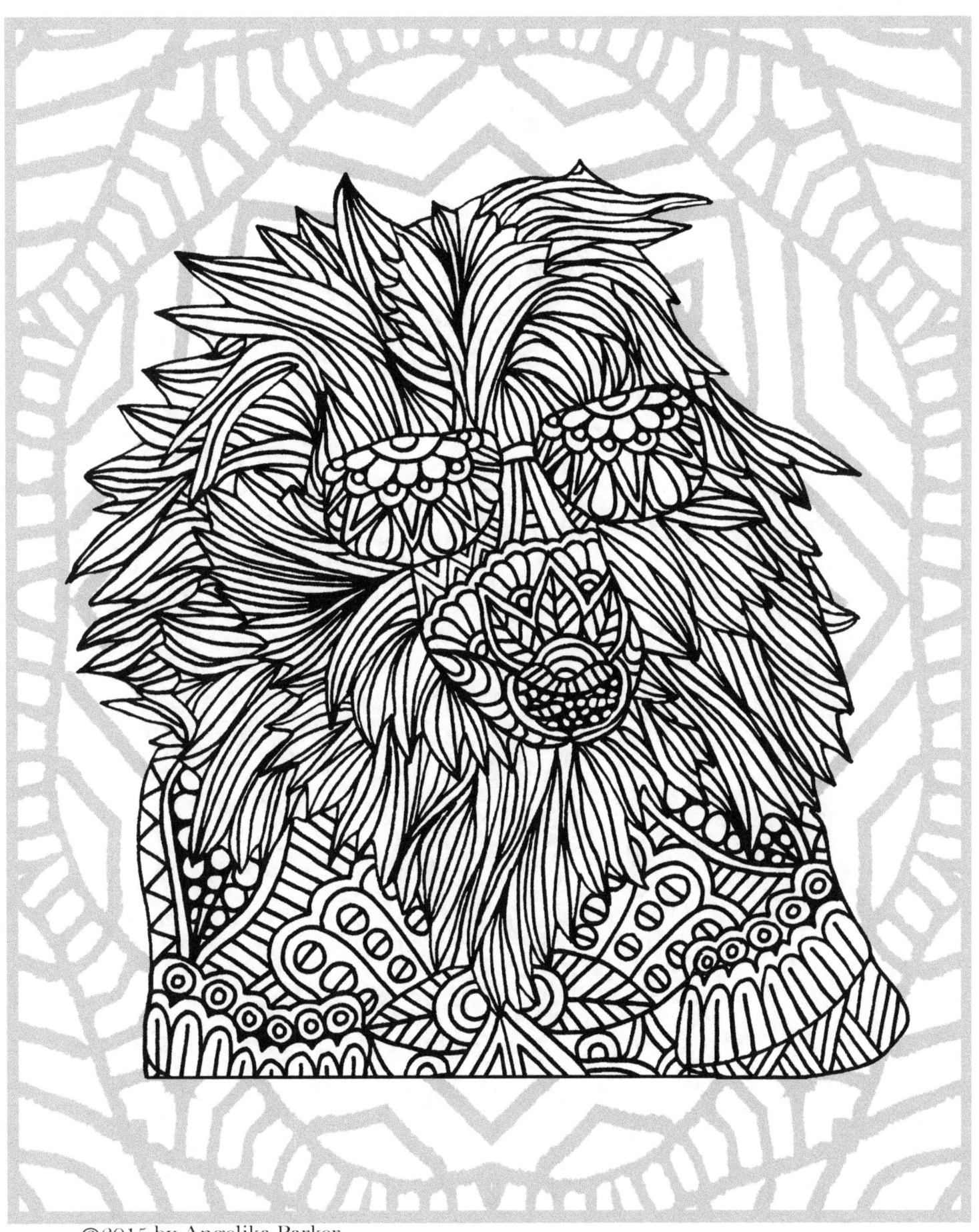

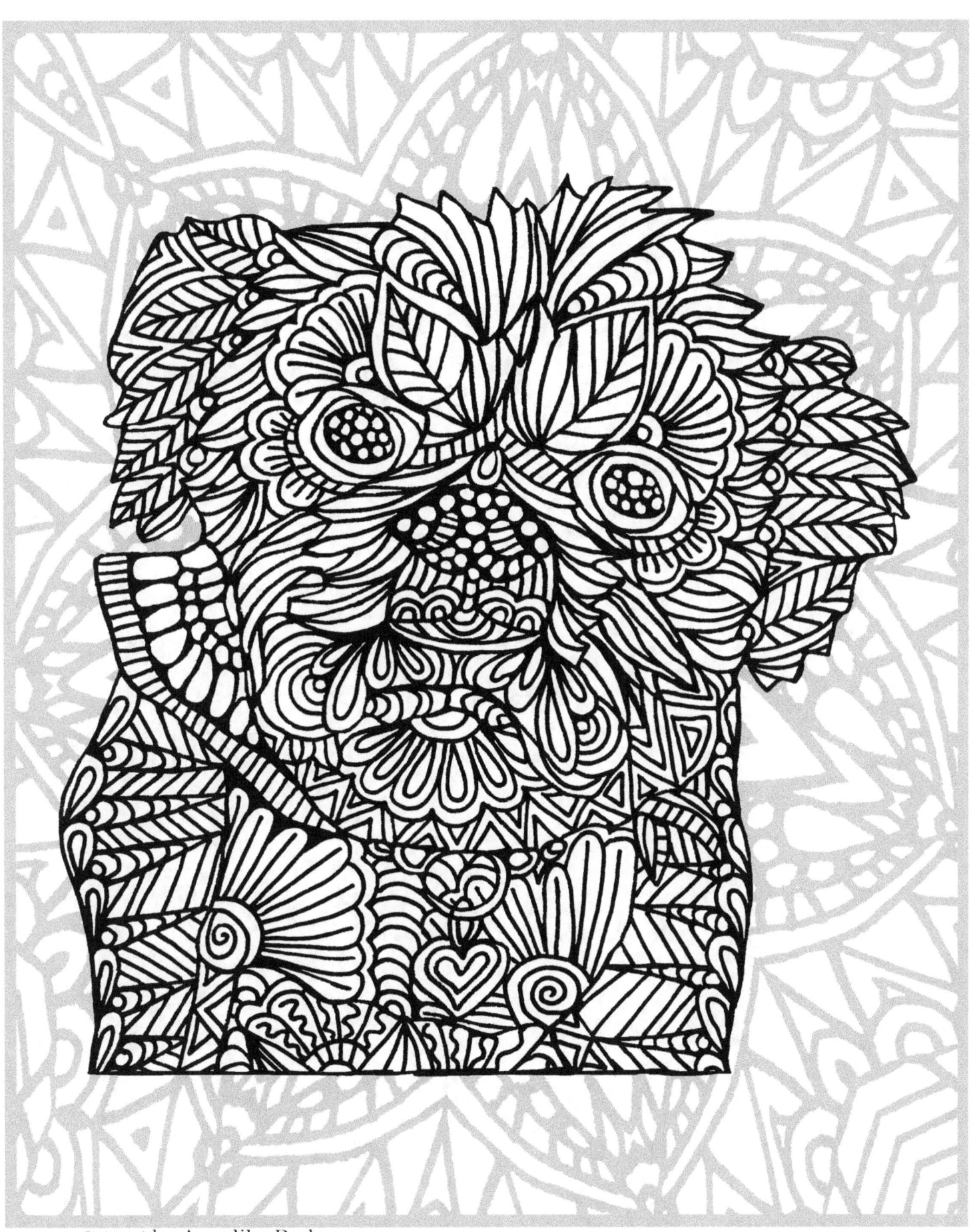

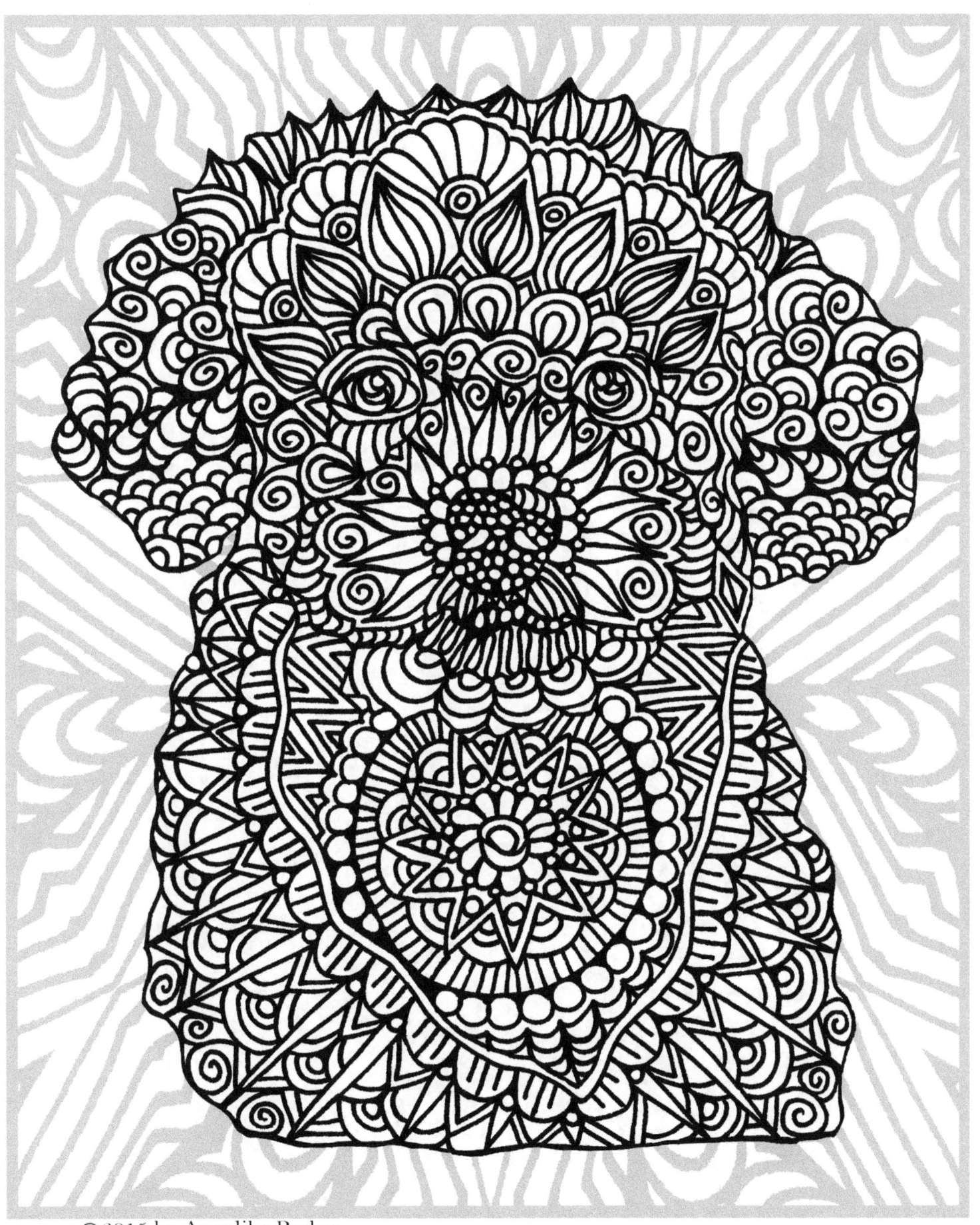

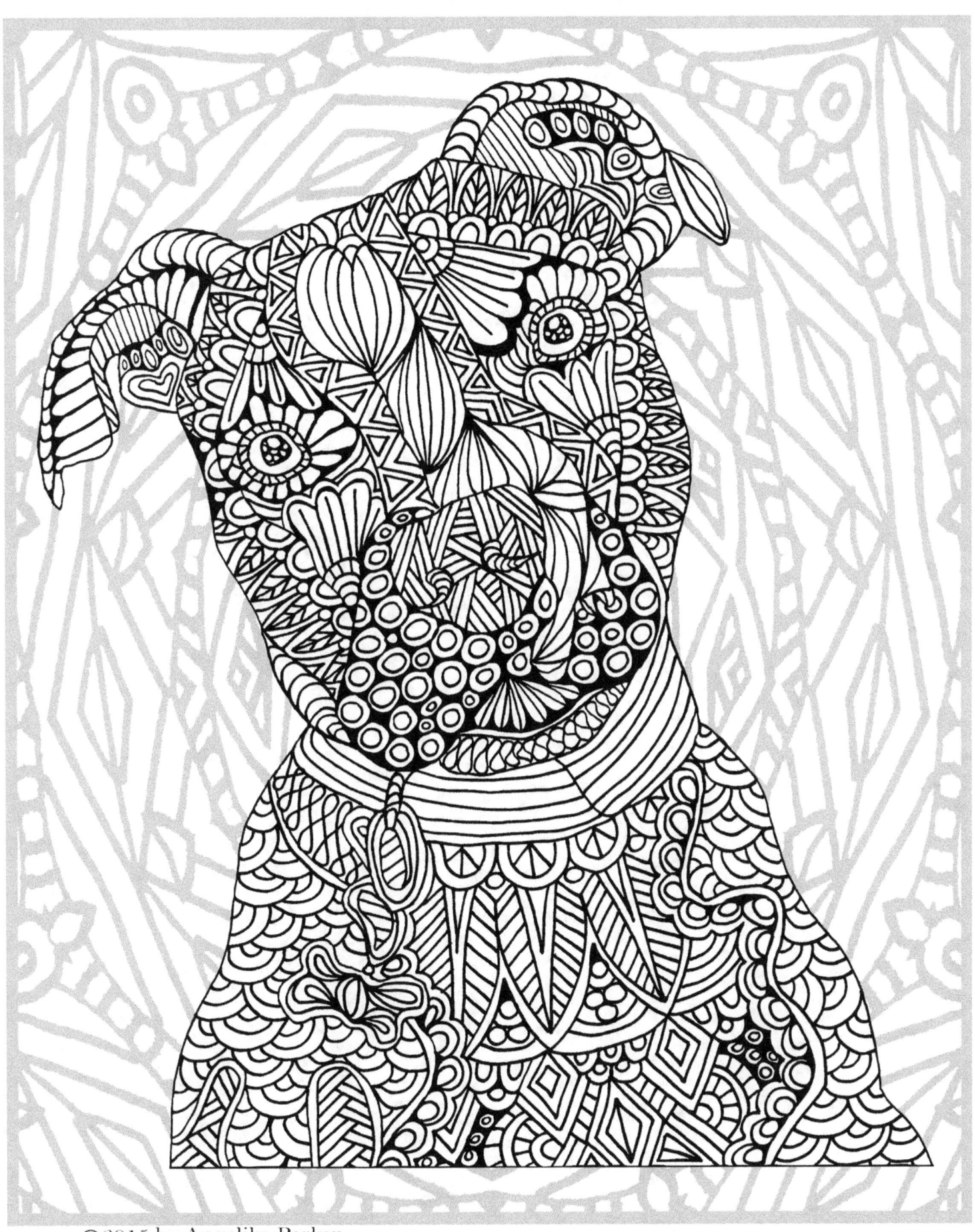

©2015 by Angelika Parker

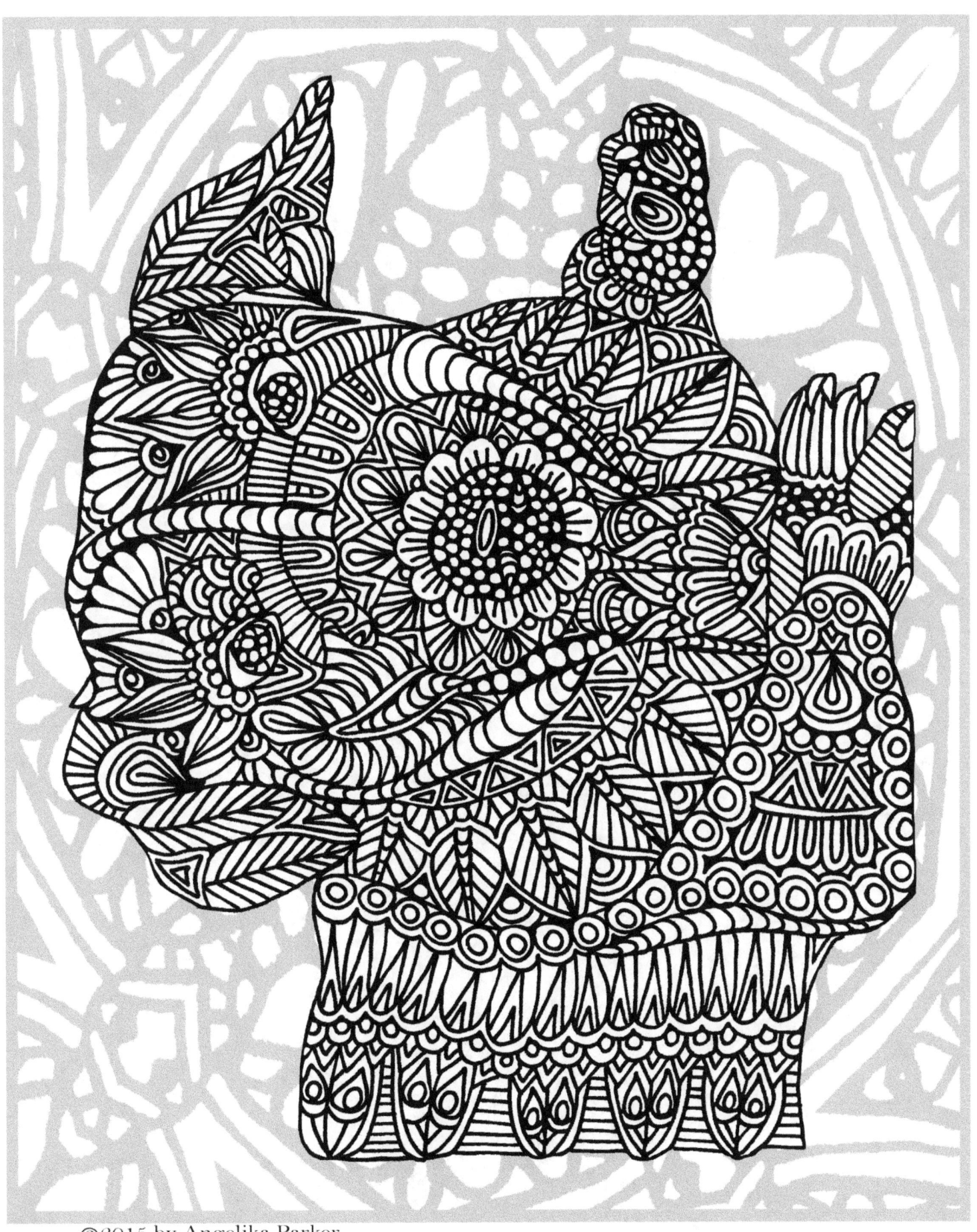

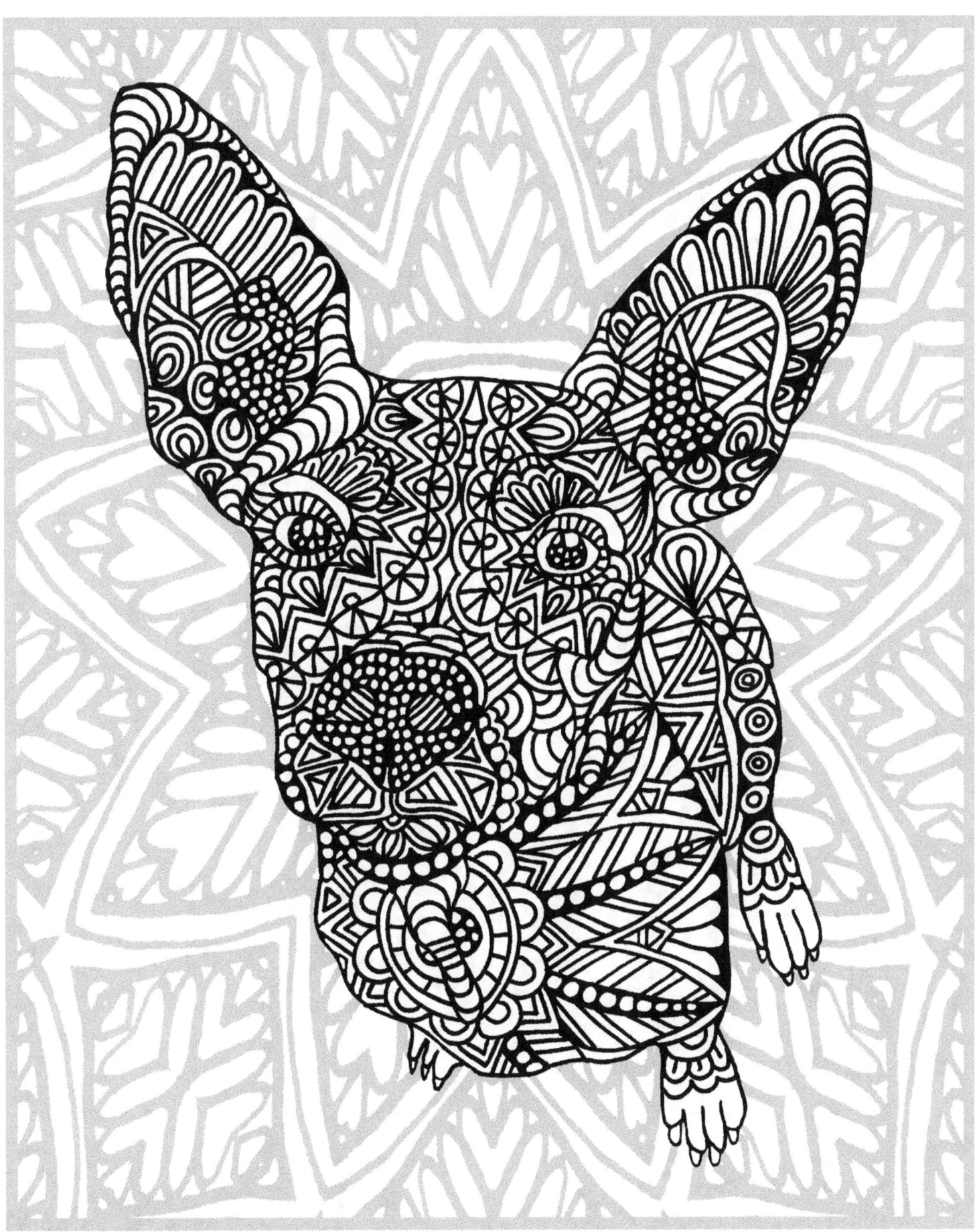

©2015 by Angelika Parker

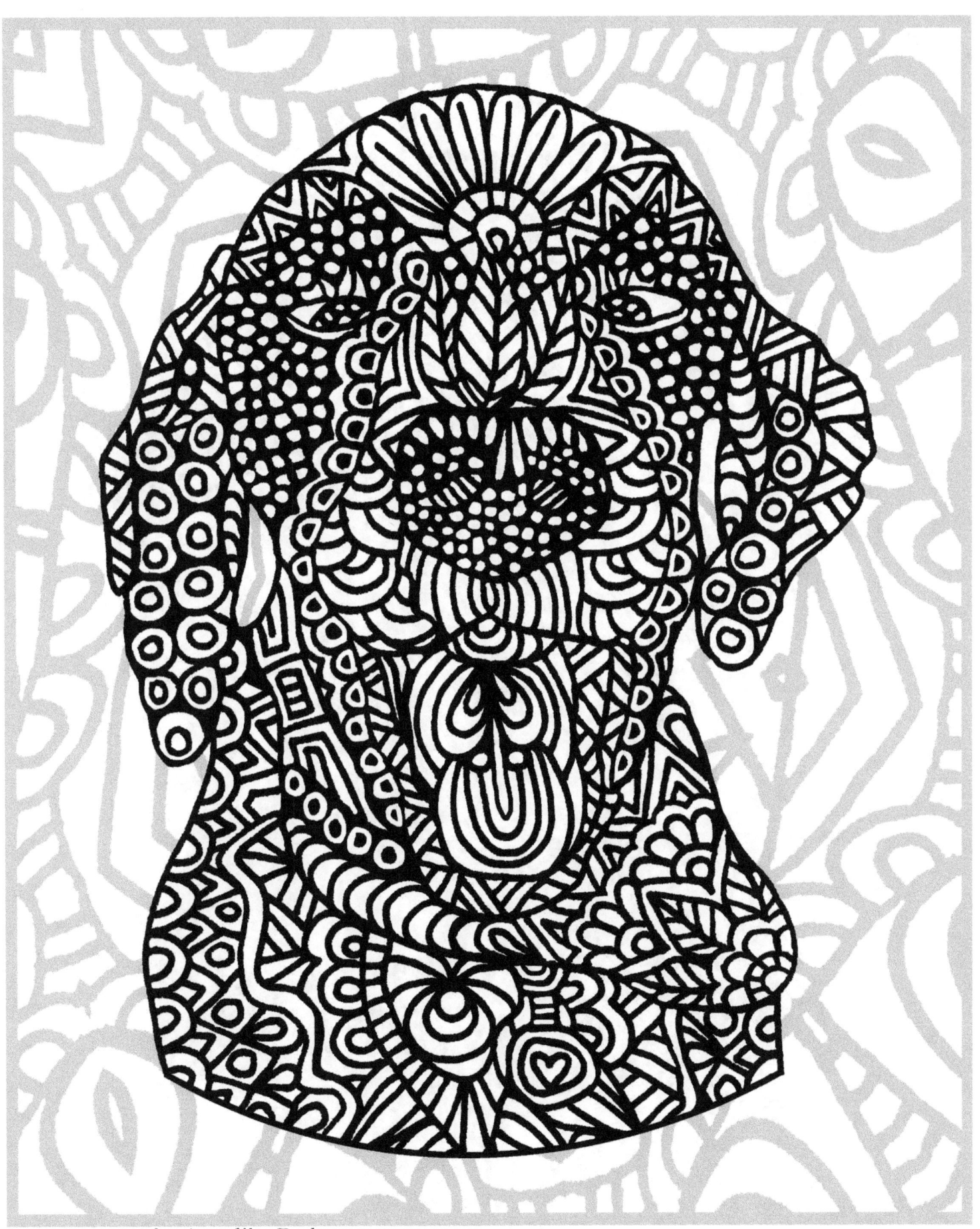

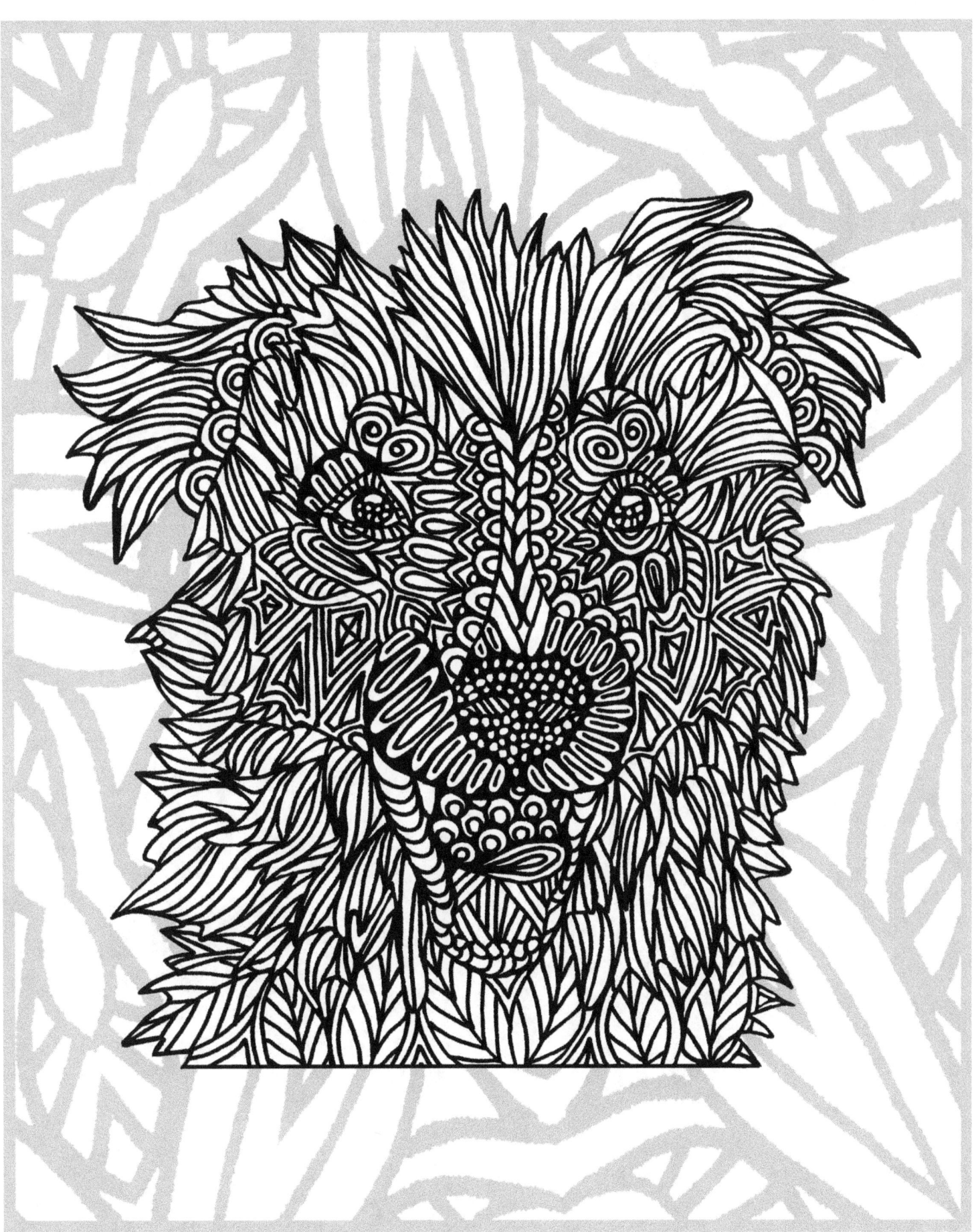

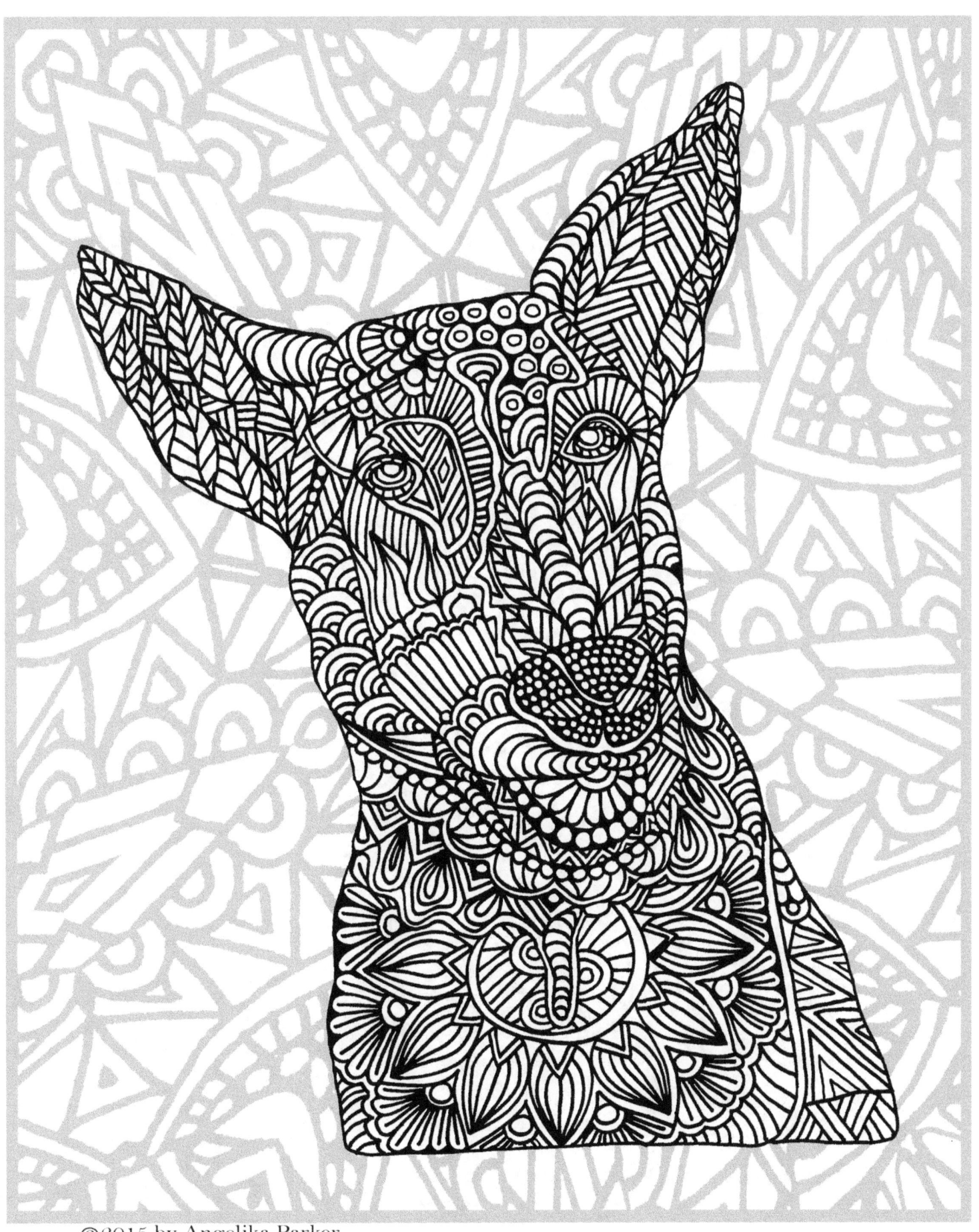

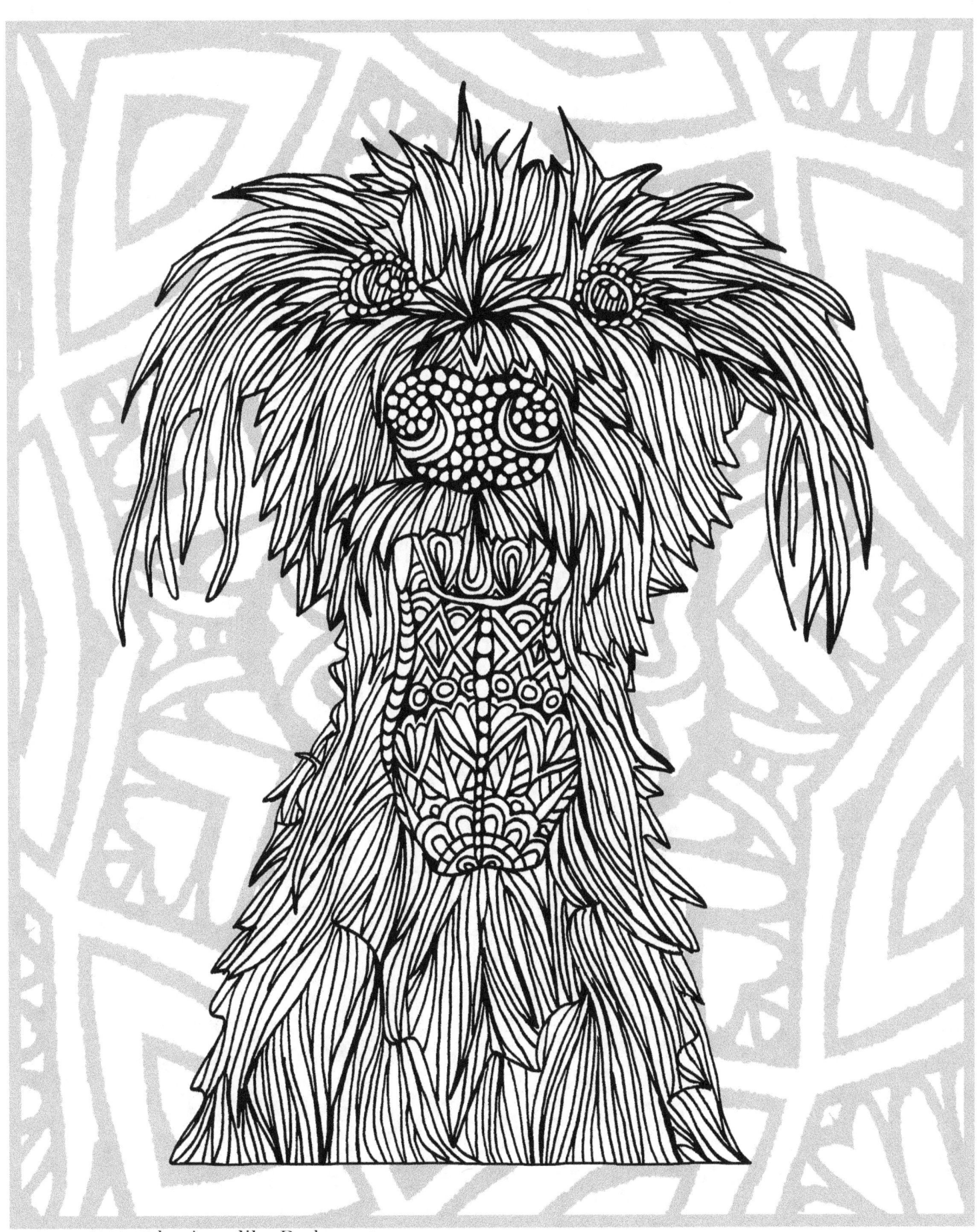

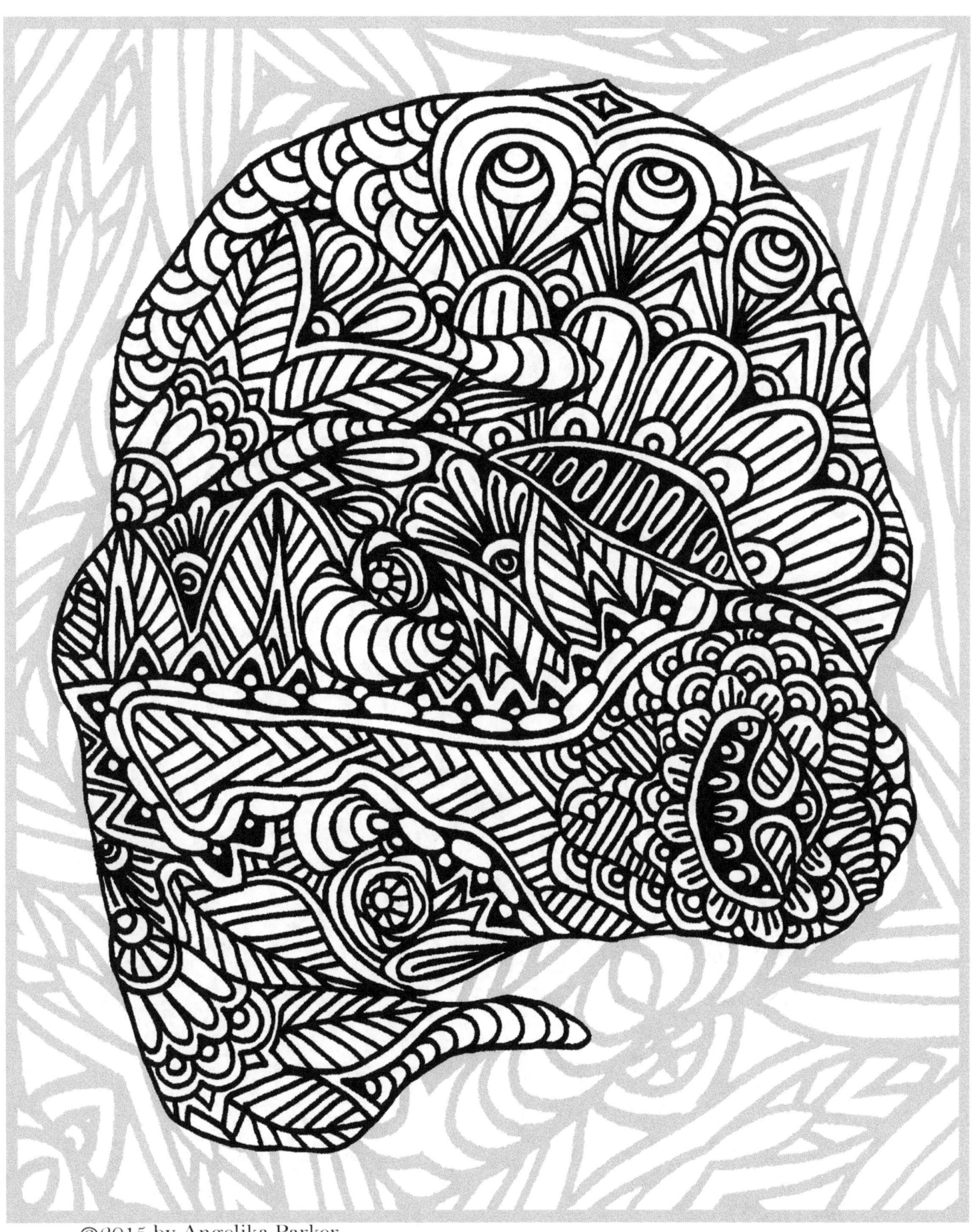

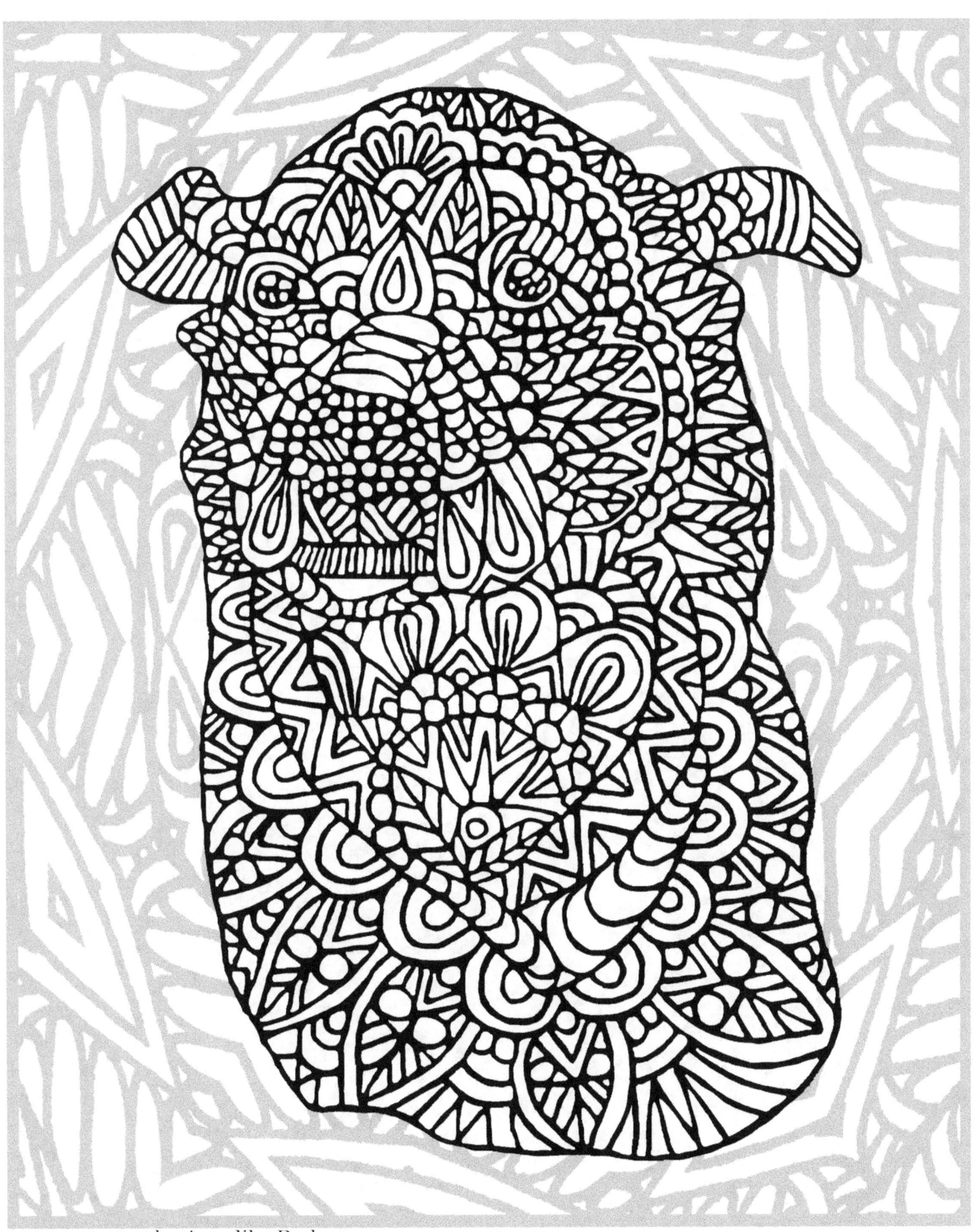

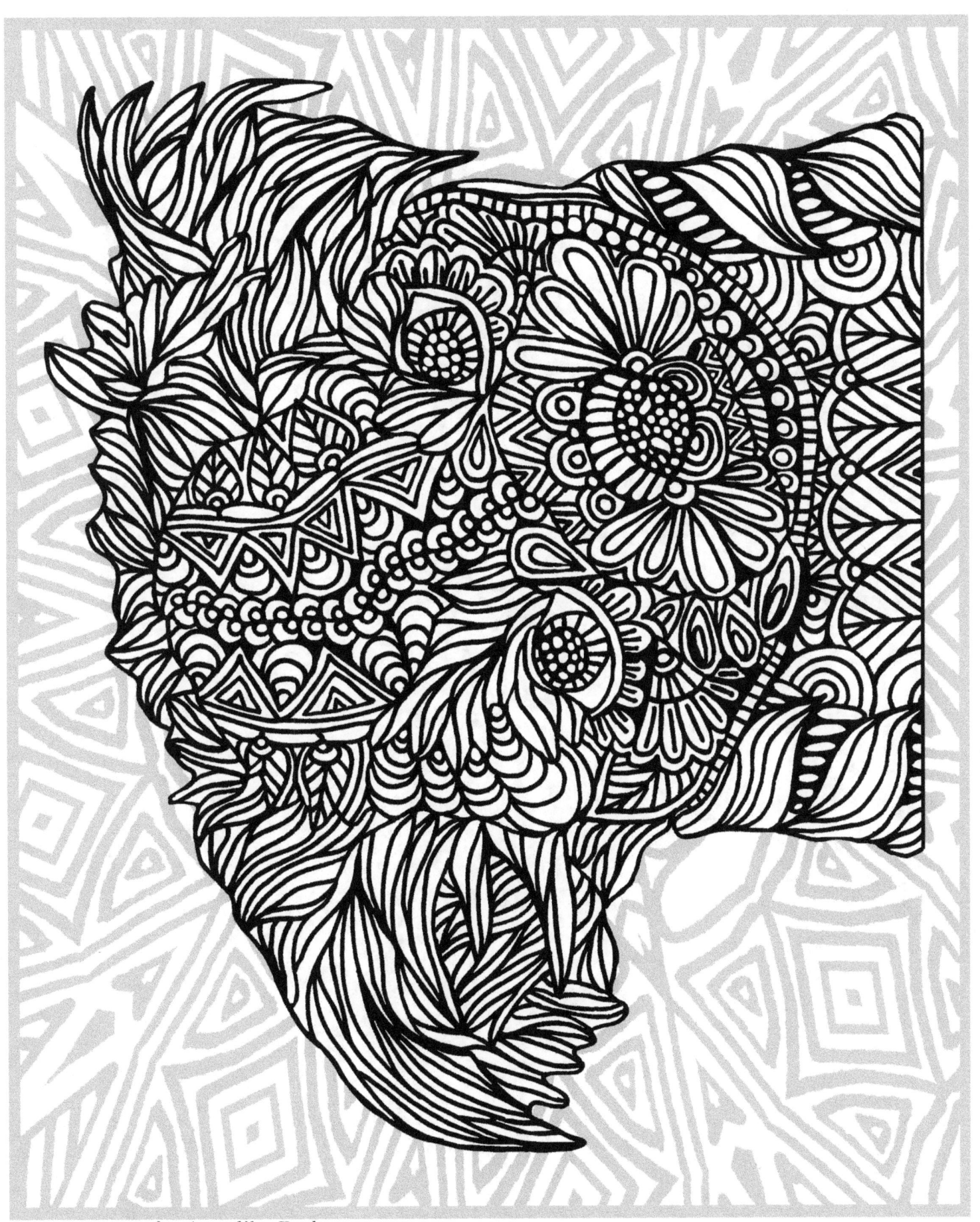

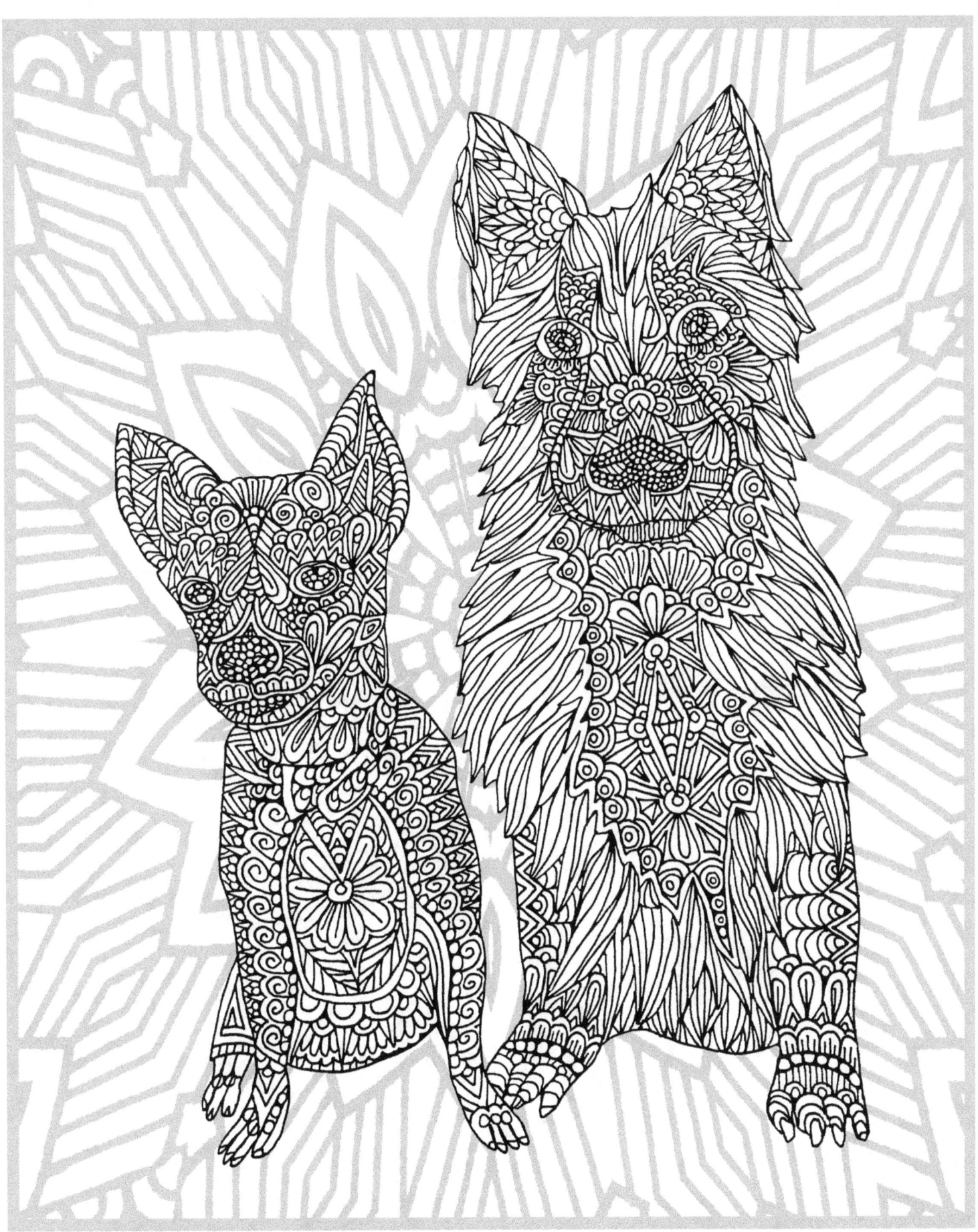

©2015 by Angelika Parker

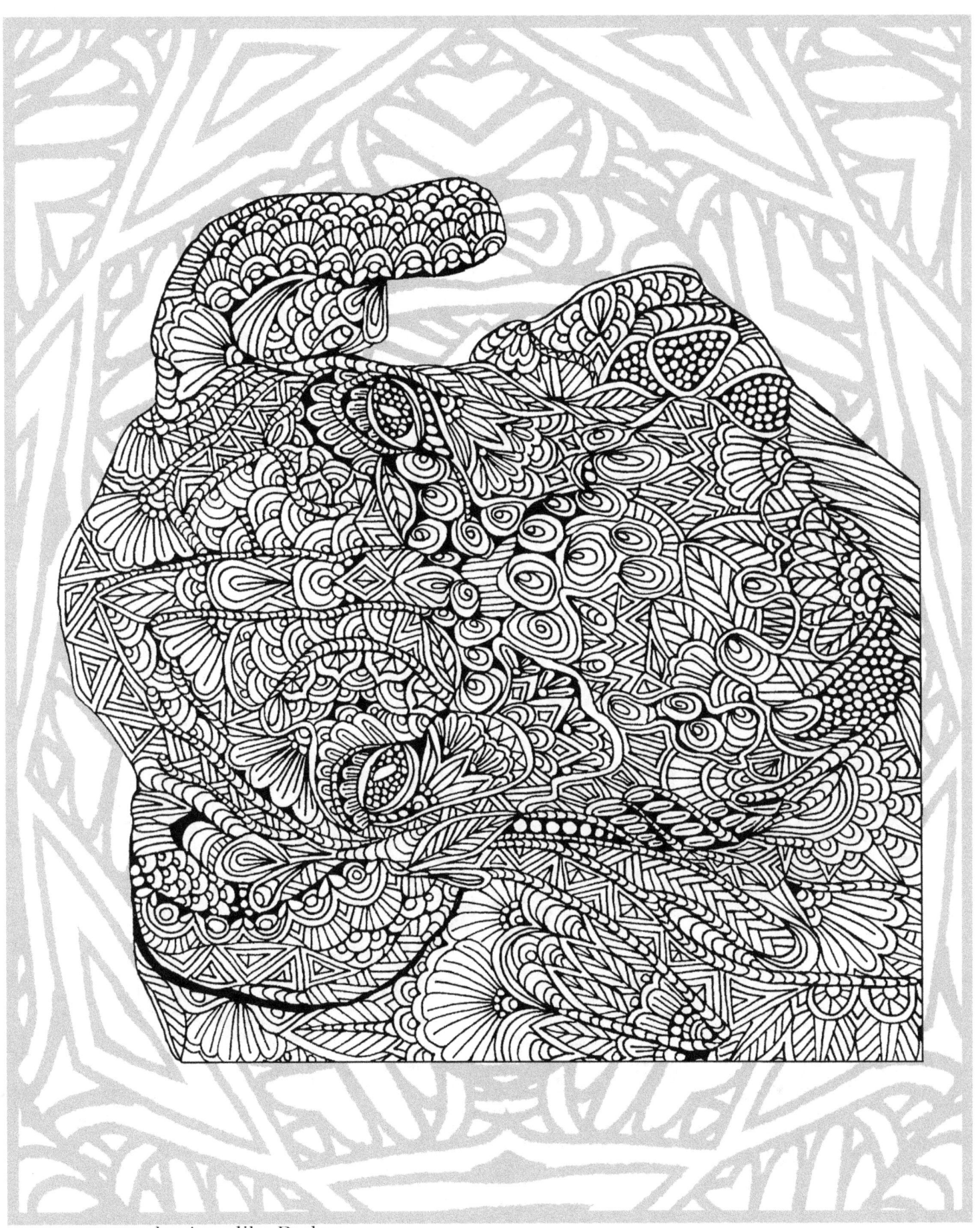

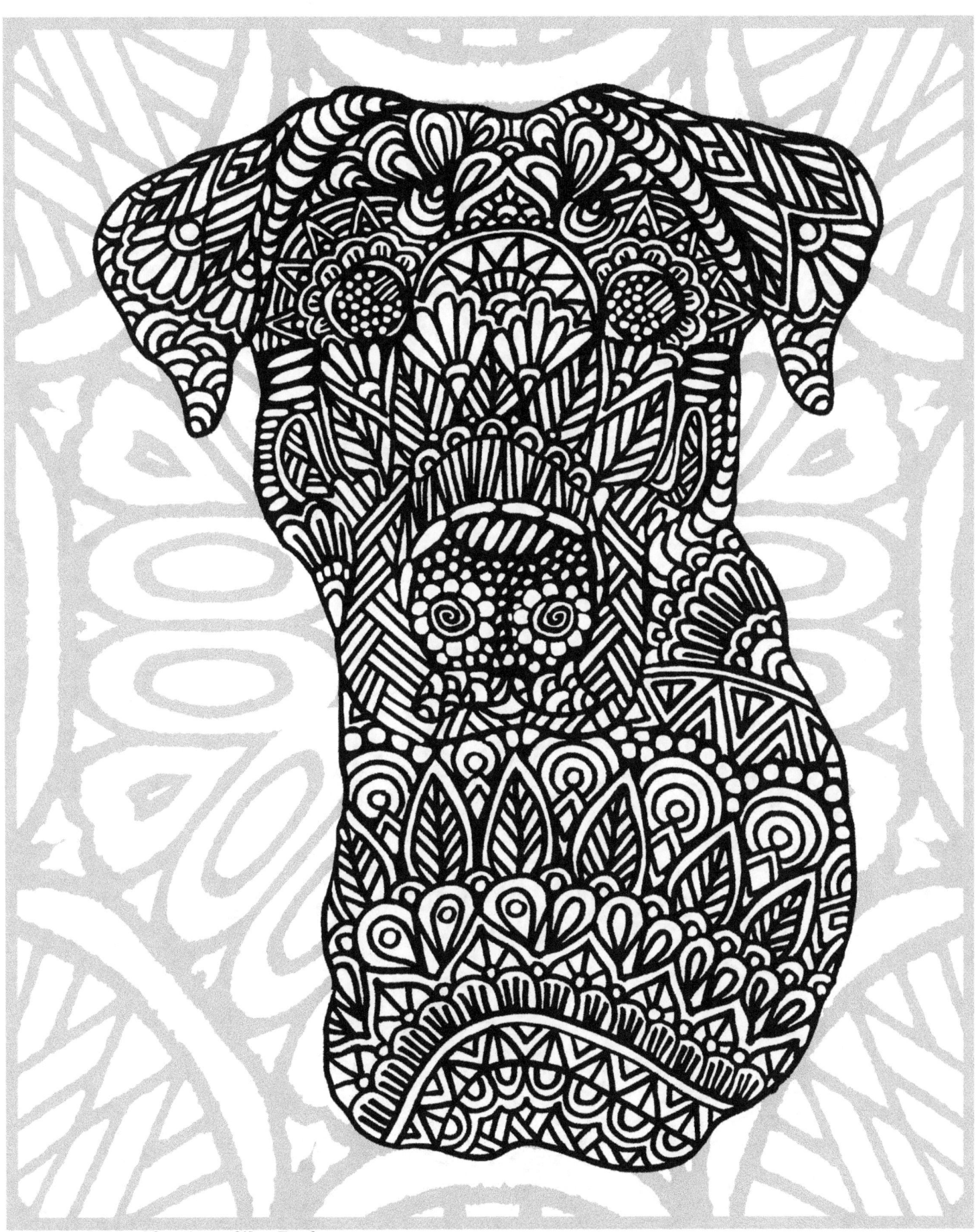

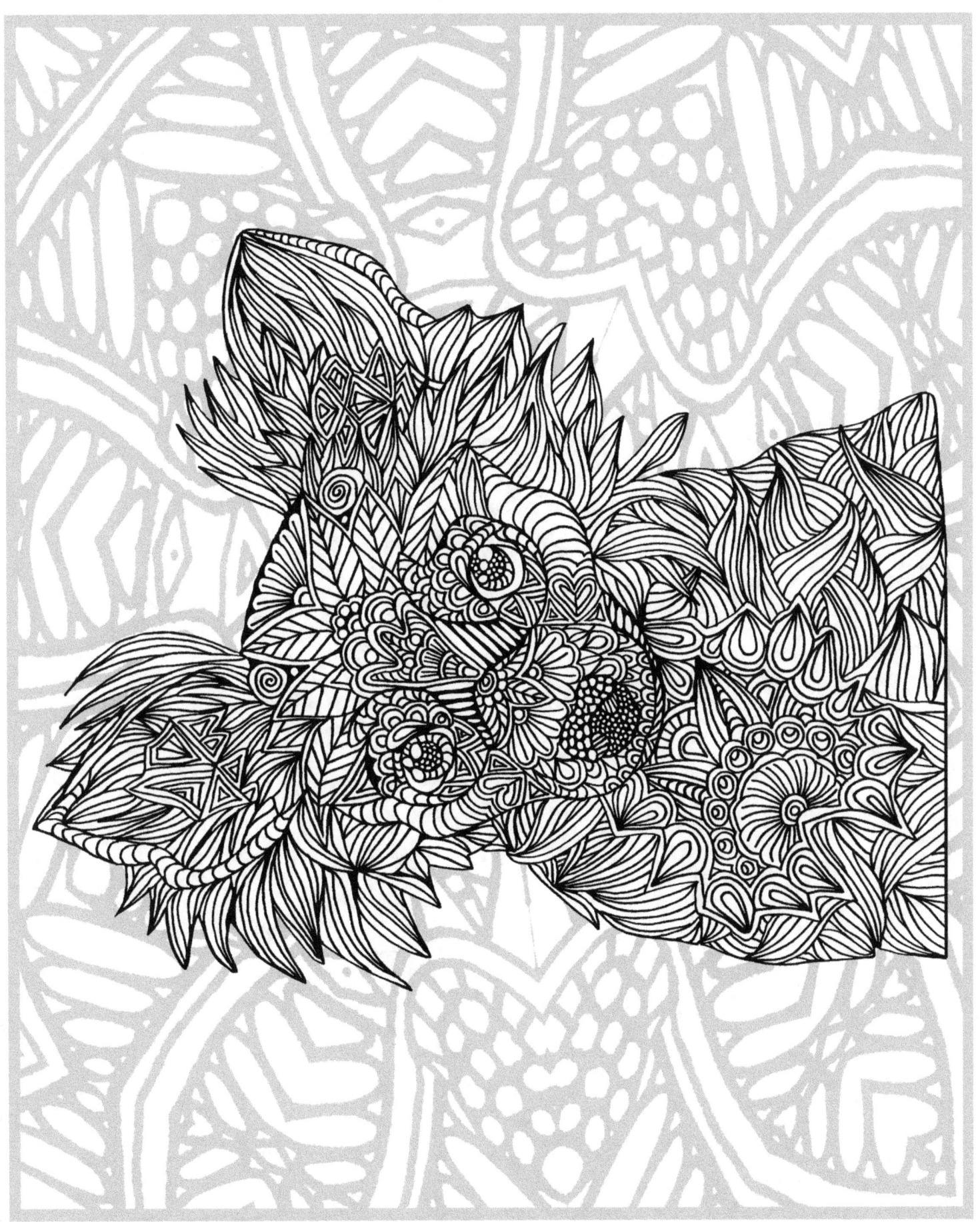

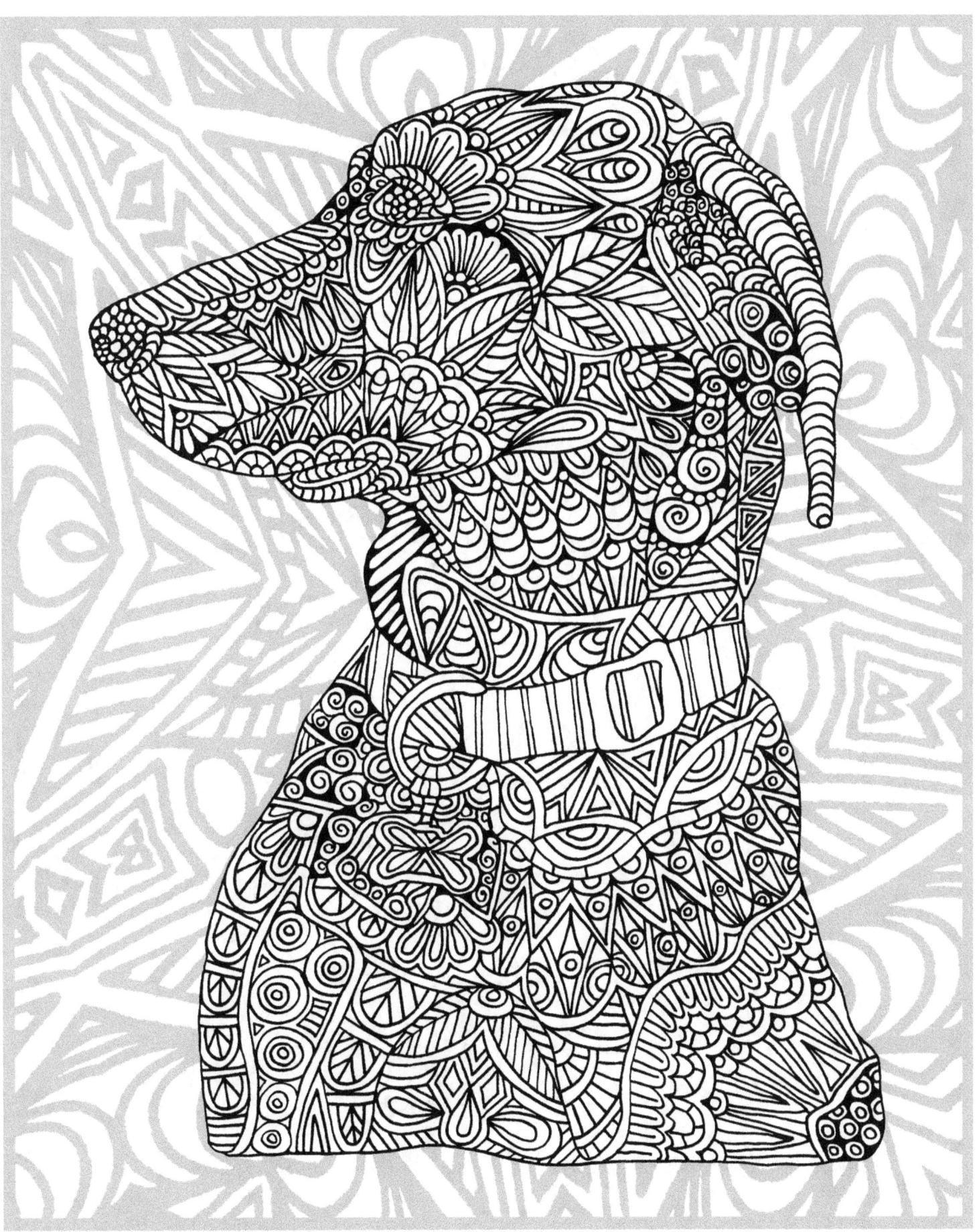

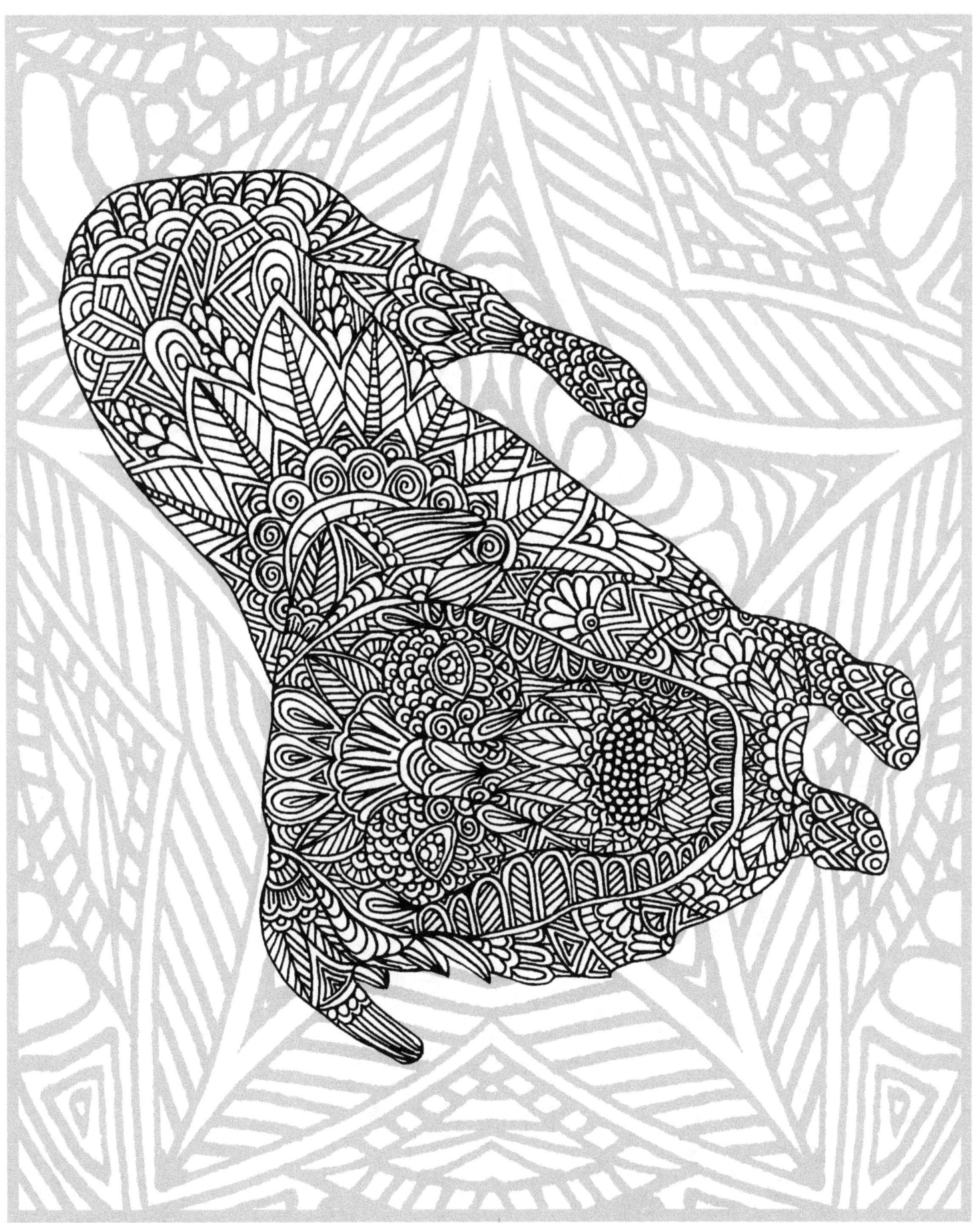

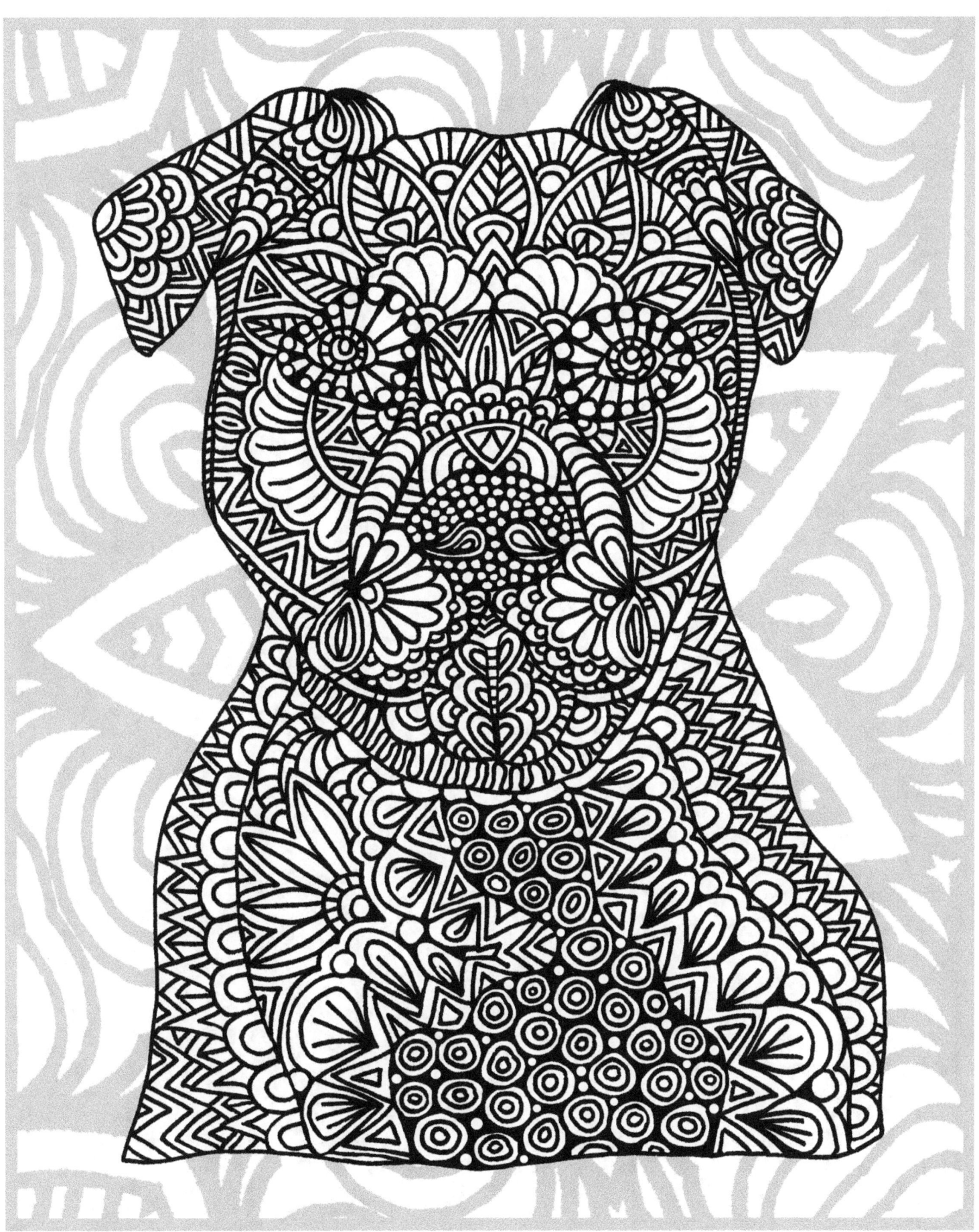

©2015 by Angelika Parker

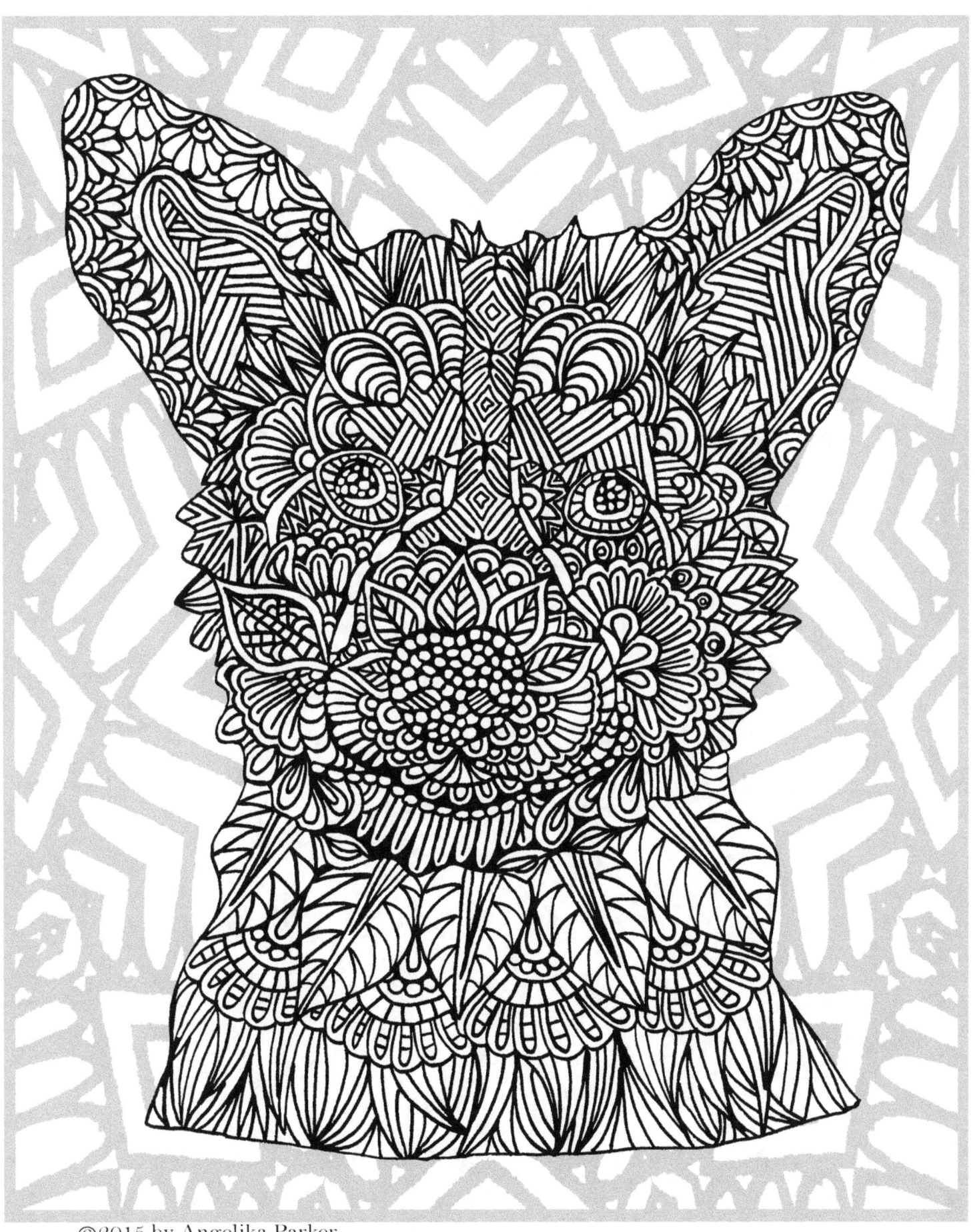

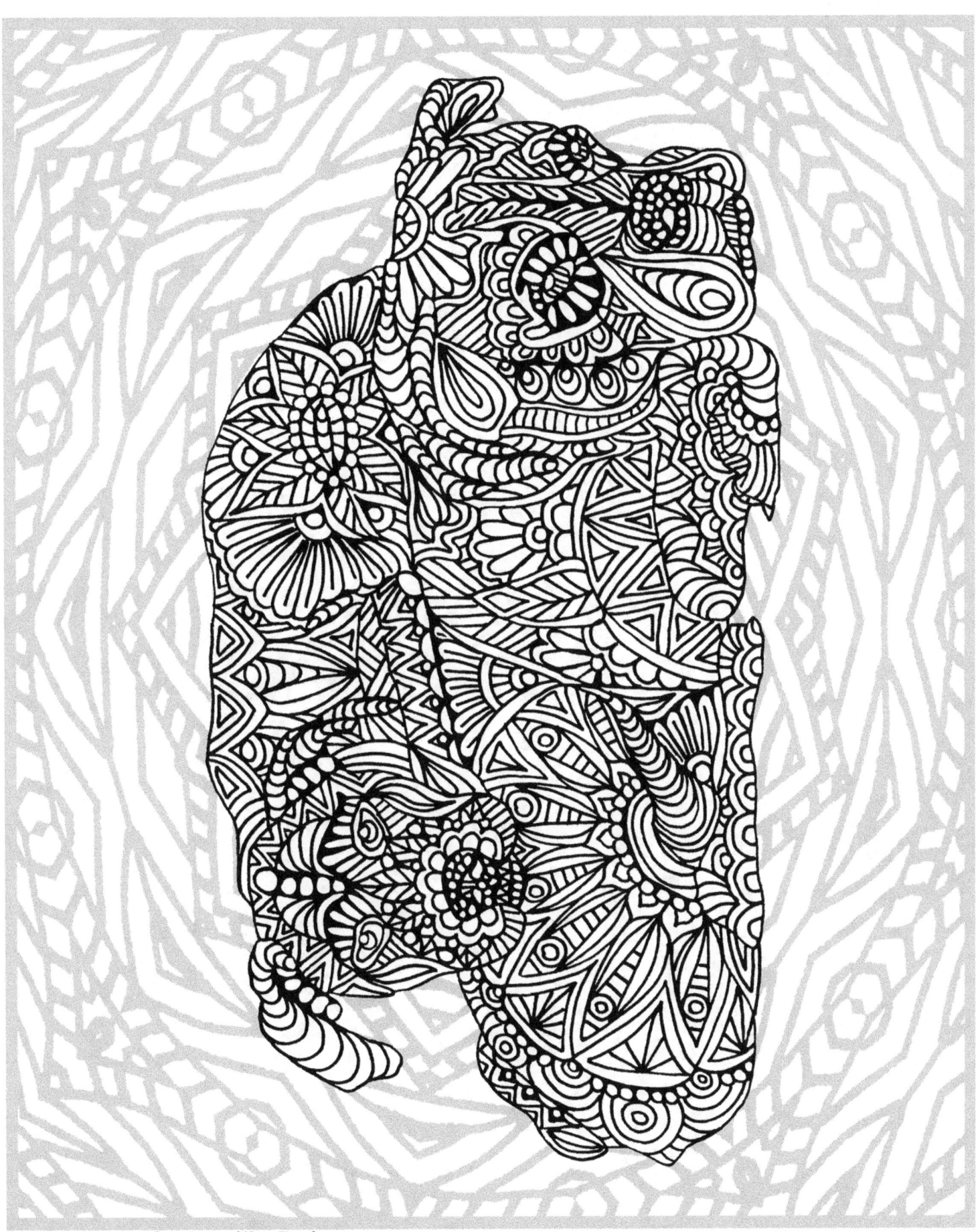

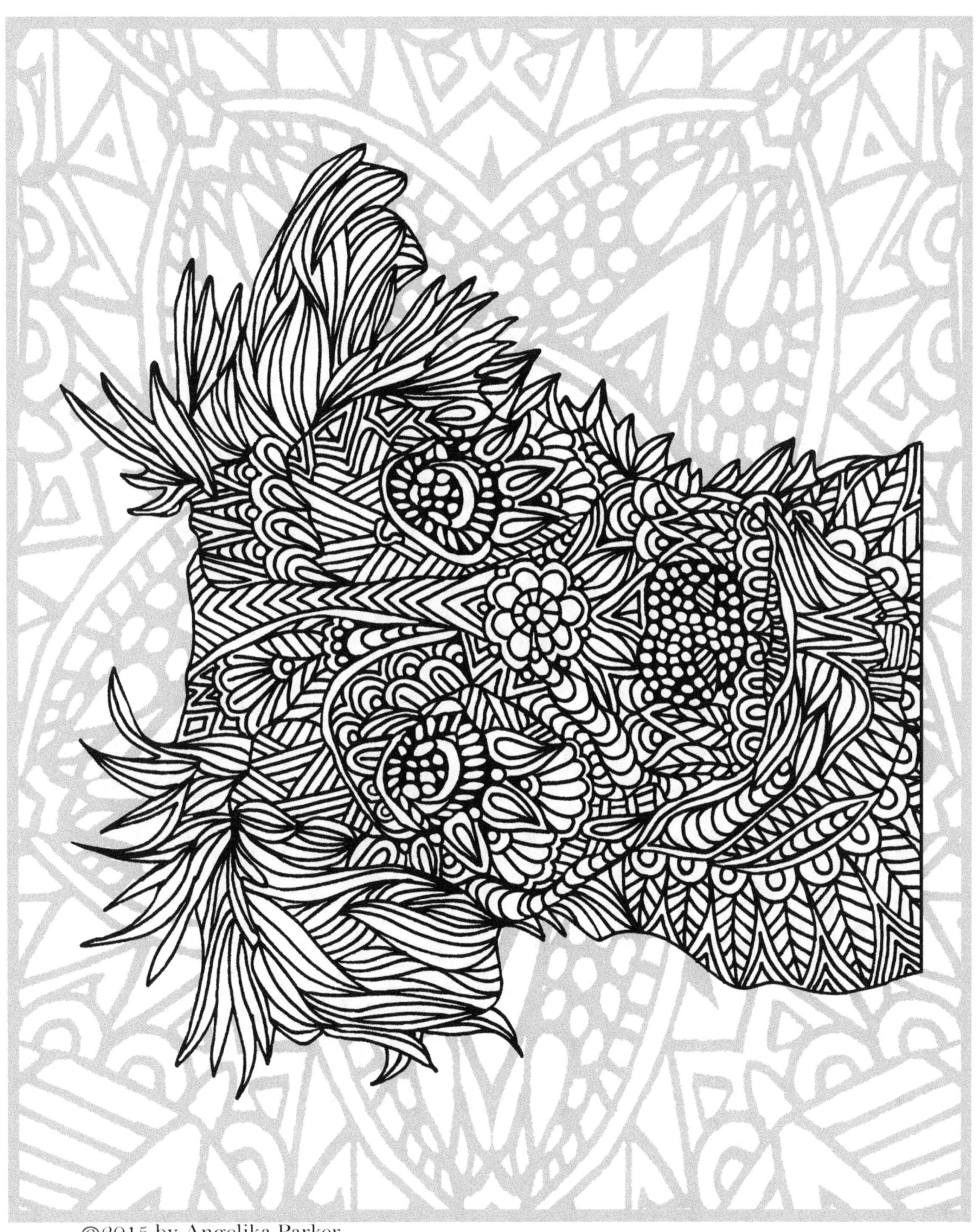

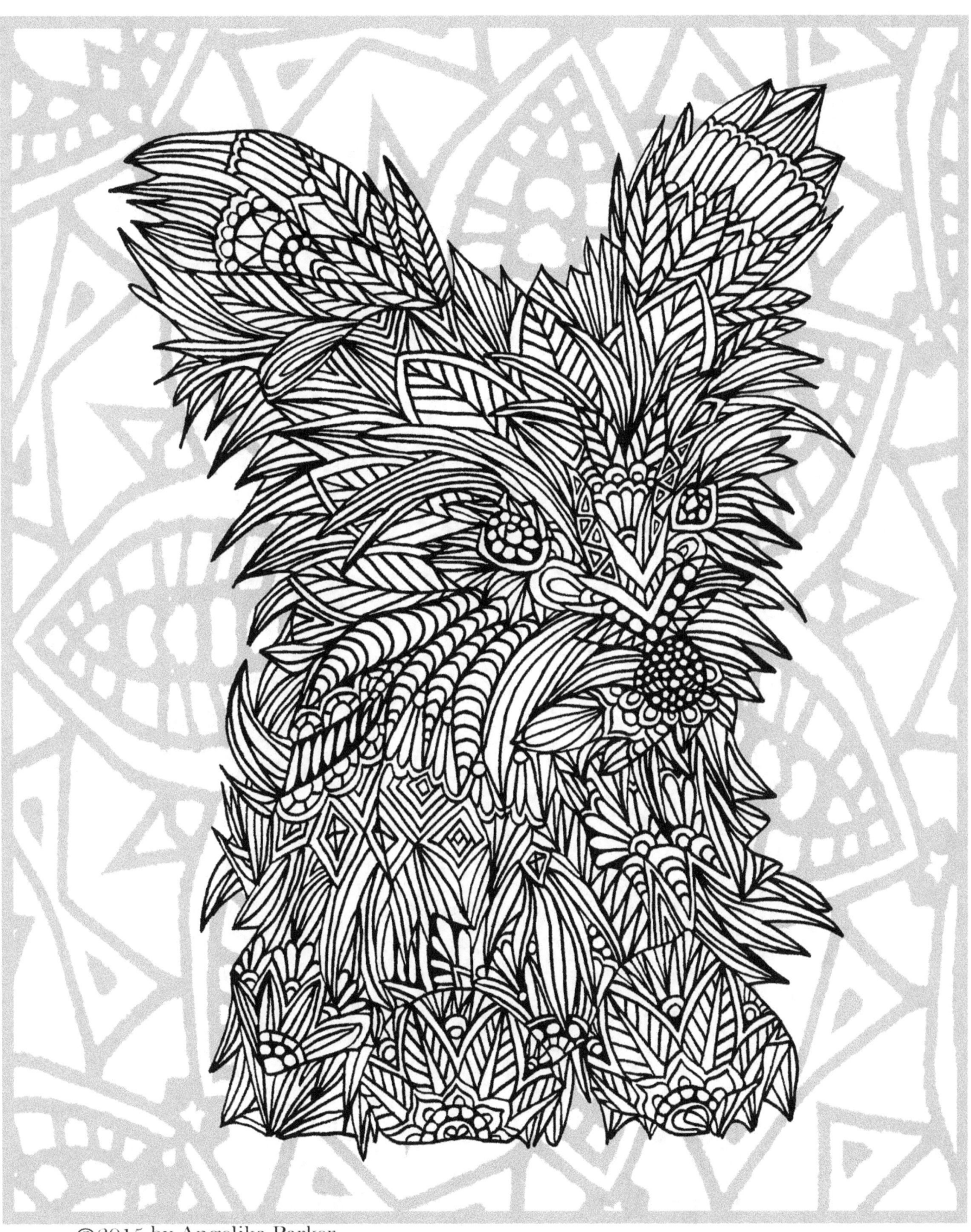

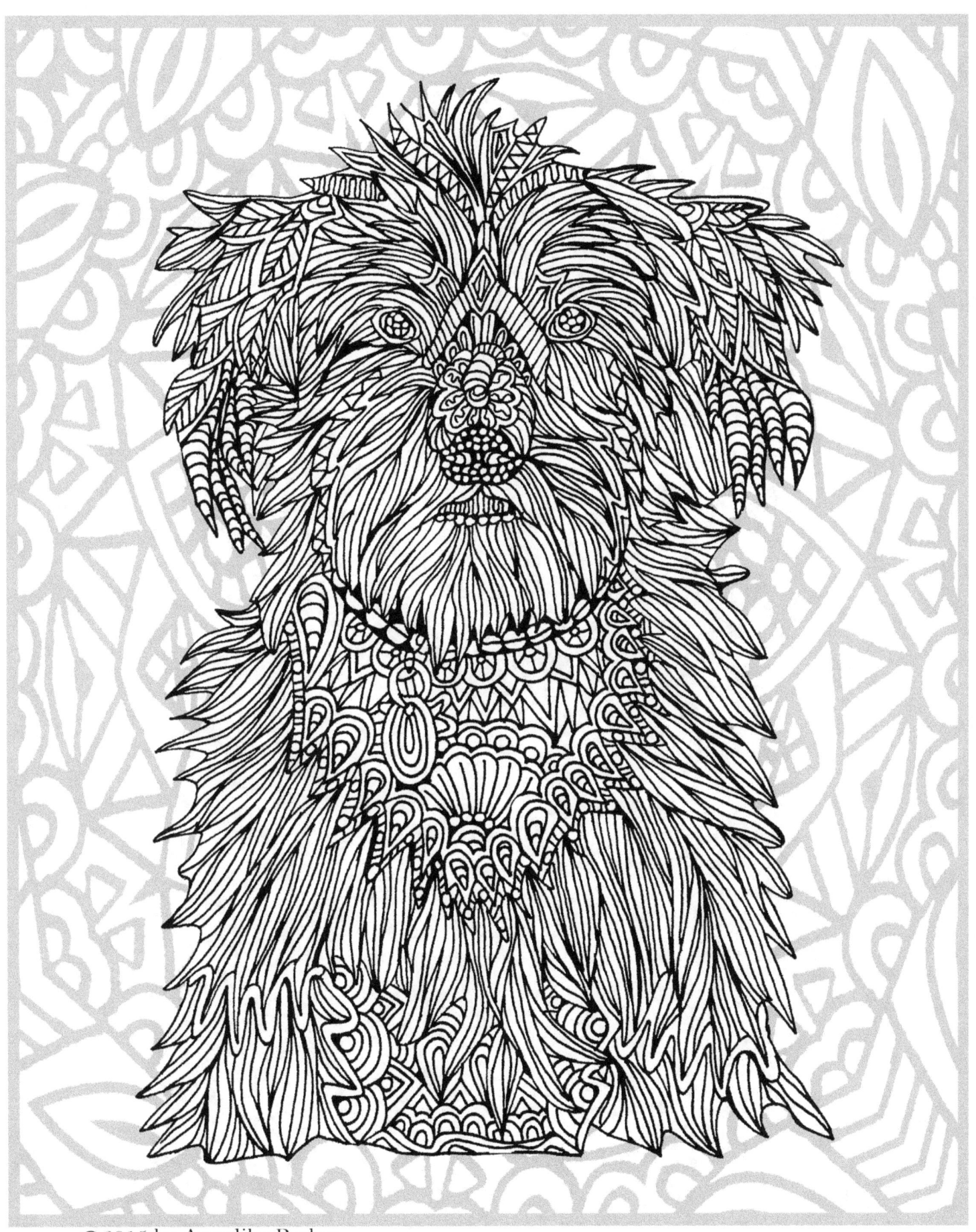

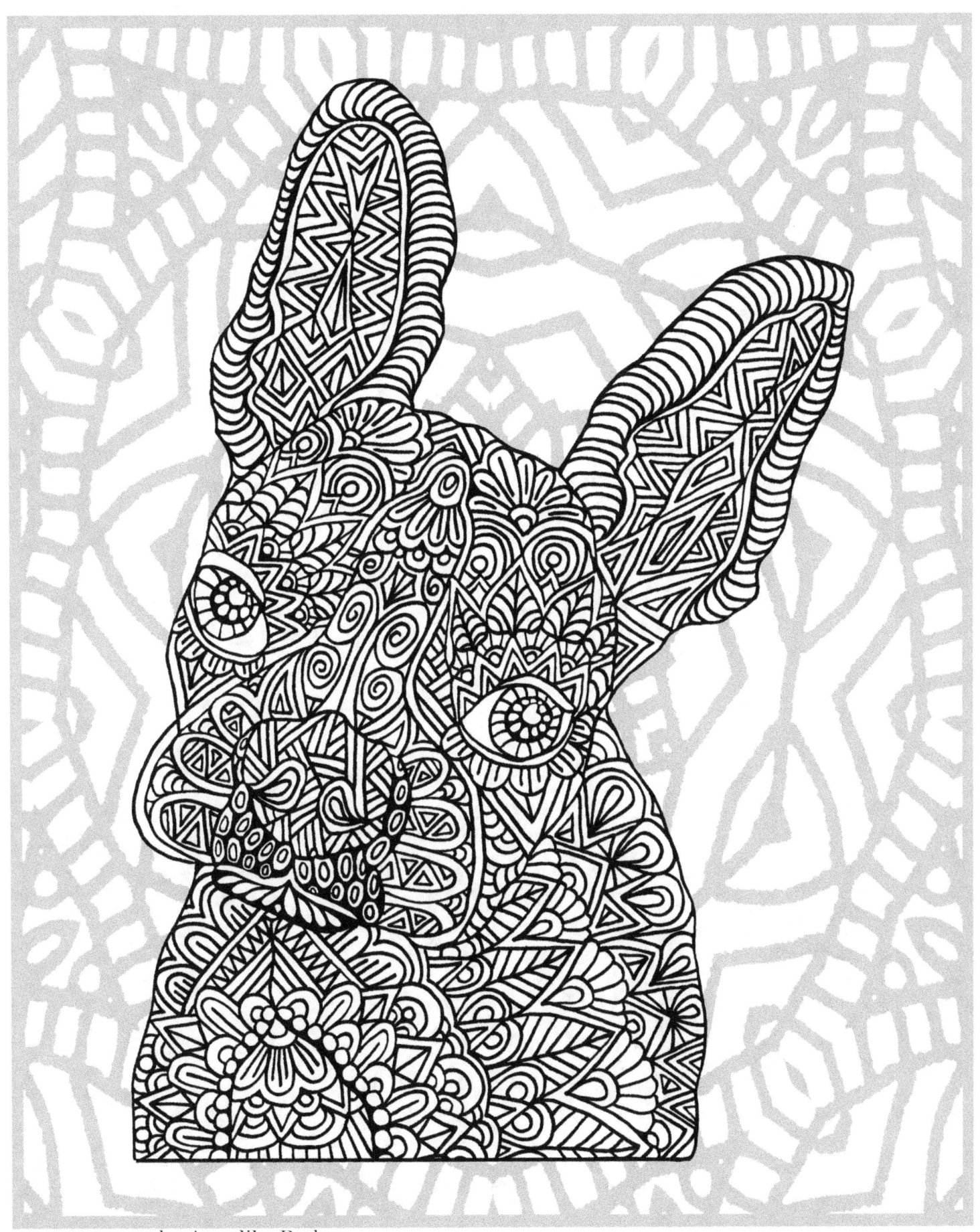

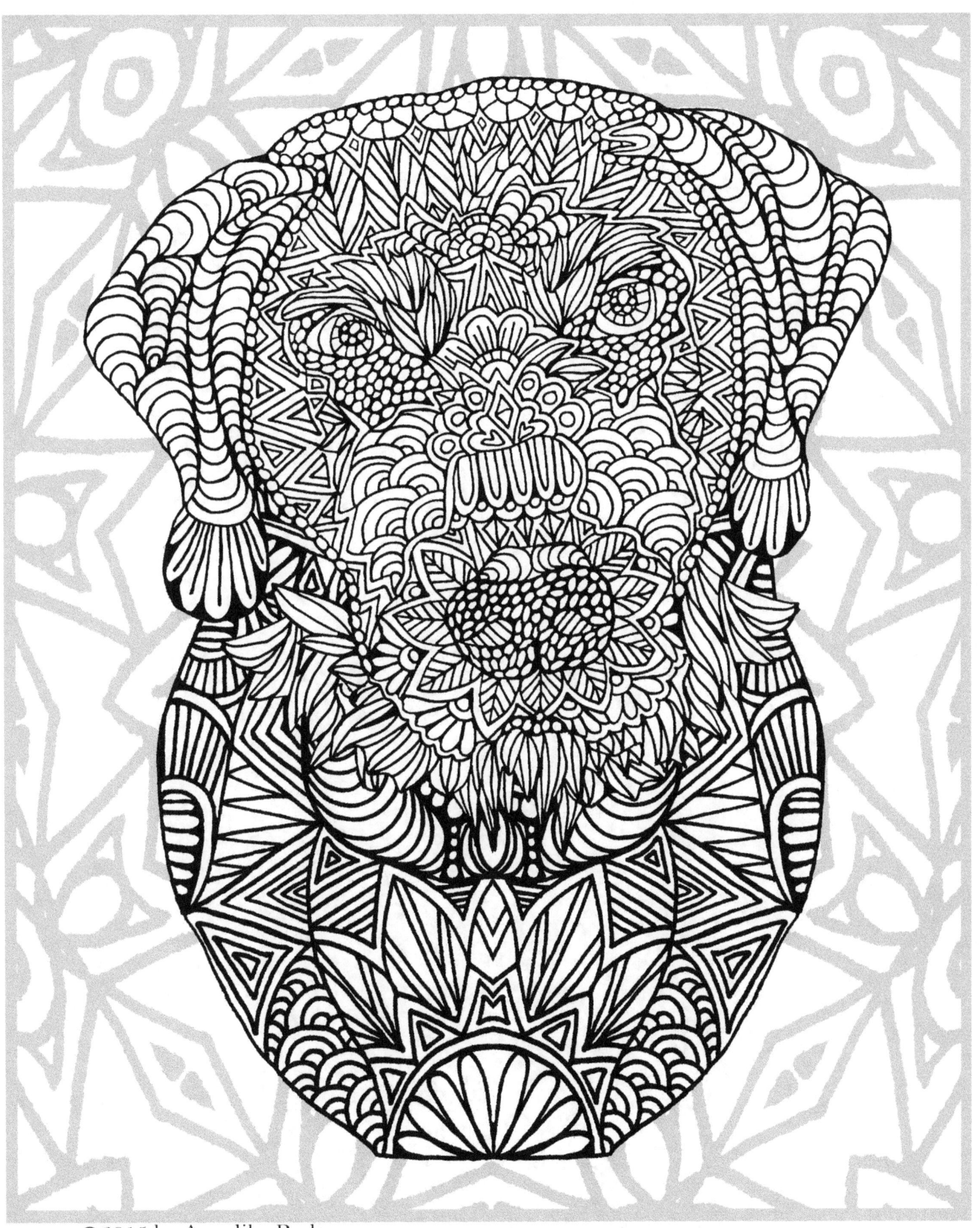

©2015 by Angelika Parker

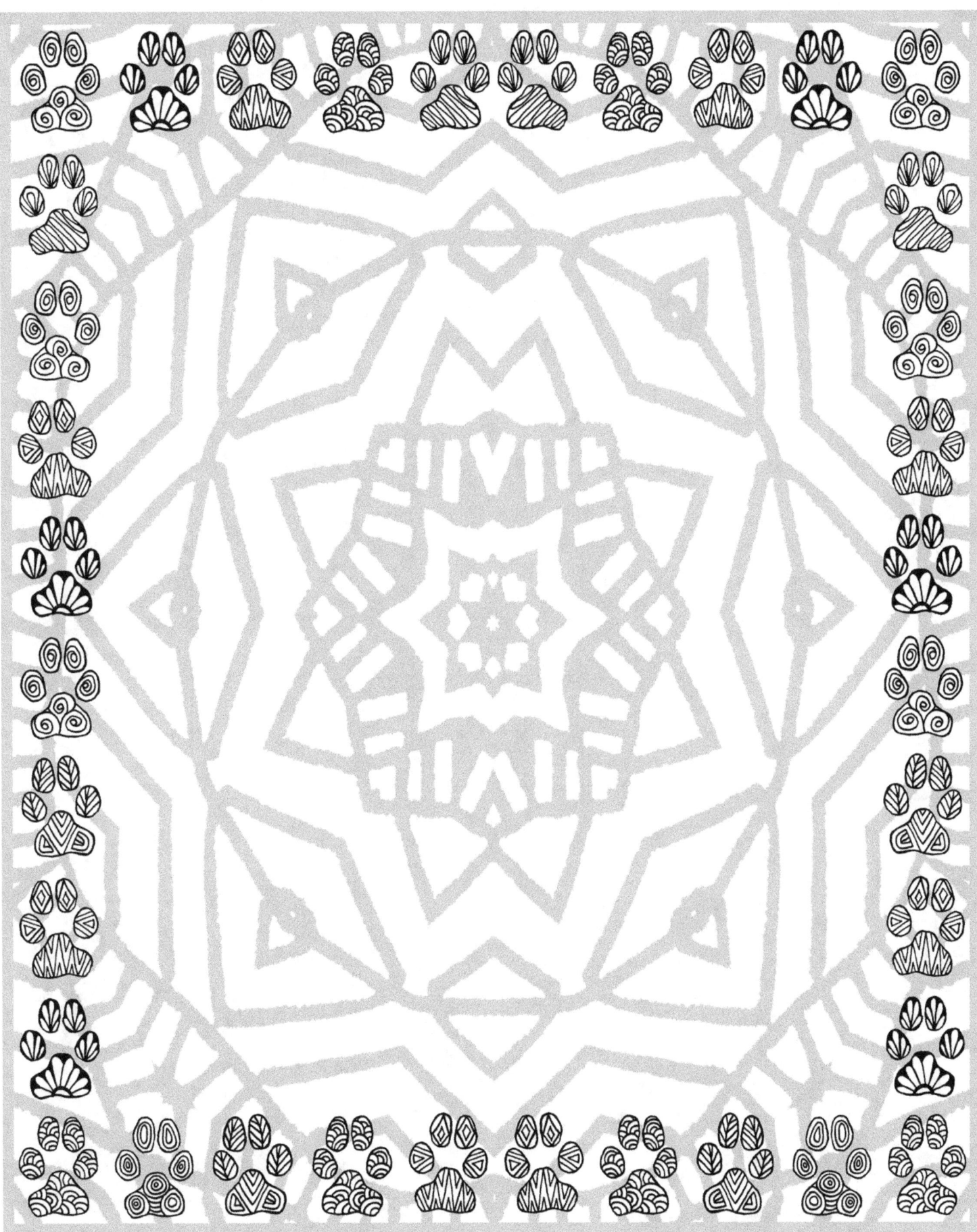

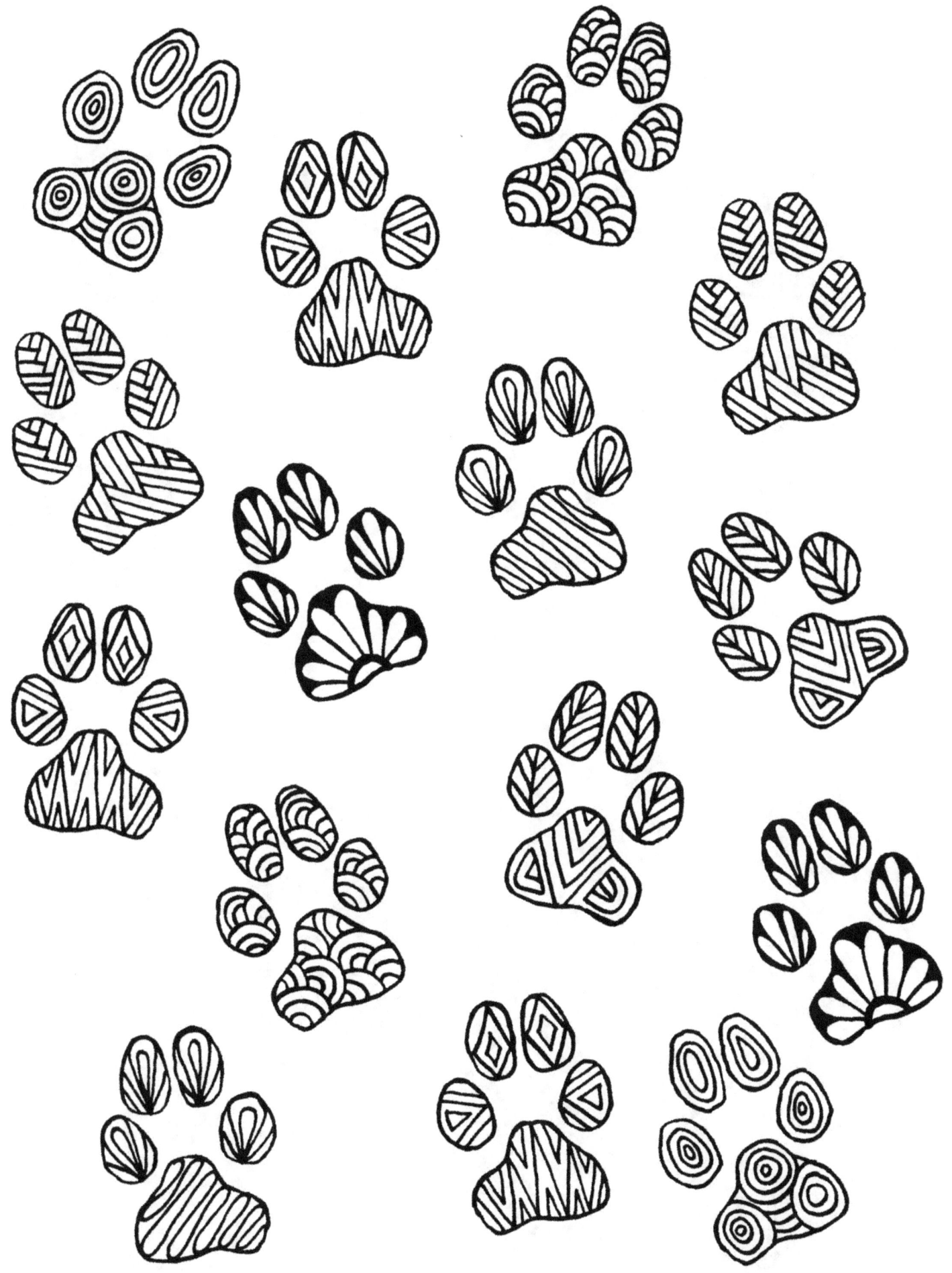

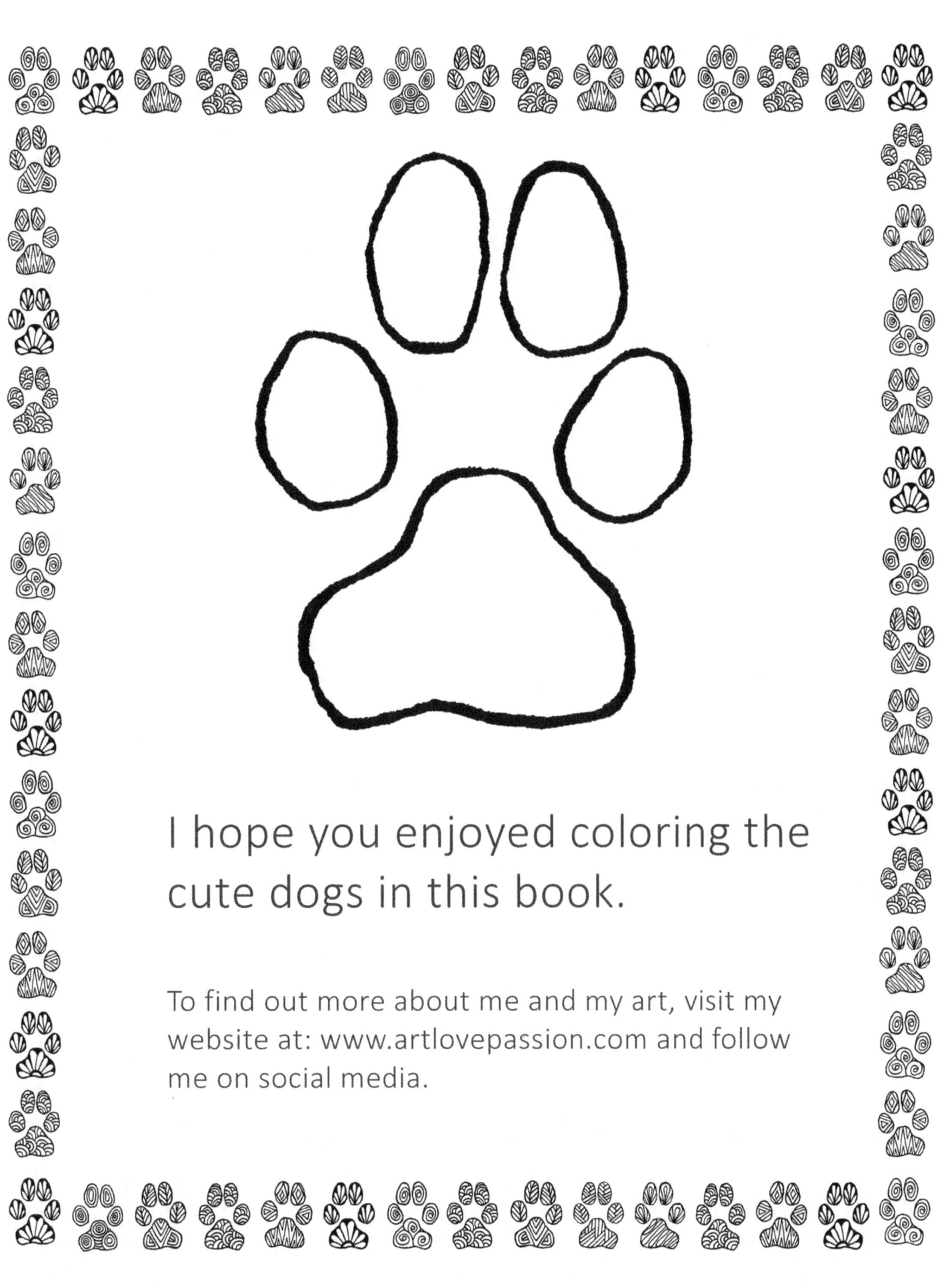

I hope you enjoyed coloring the cute dogs in this book.

To find out more about me and my art, visit my website at: www.artlovepassion.com and follow me on social media.